PHOTO ART THERAPY

ABOUT THE AUTHORS

Jerry L. Fryrear, Ph.D., ATR, is a clinical psychologist and art therapist. He is professor of psychology at the University of Houston-Clear Lake and has a private practice in psychology and art therapy. Dr. Fryrear has published three books and numerous chapters and articles on the expressive arts in therapy. He is on the editorial board of *The Arts in Psychotherapy.*

Irene E. Corbit, Ph.D., ATR, LPC is an art therapist in private practice in Houston. She conducts workshops on the expressive arts in therapy, in addition to her work with private clients. Dr. Corbit is on the editorial board of *The Arts in Psychotherapy* and is an adjunct instructor at the University of Houston-Clear Lake. She is coordinator of the School of Expressive Arts at the C. G. Jung Educational Center in Houston, Texas.

PHOTO ART THERAPY
A Jungian Perspective

By

JERRY L. FRYREAR, Ph.D., A.T.R.

and

IRENE E. CORBIT, Ph.D., A.T.R.

With a Foreword by
Shaun McNiff

CHARLES C THOMAS • PUBLISHER
Springfield • Illinois • U.S.A.

Published and Distributed Throughout the World by

CHARLES C THOMAS • PUBLISHER
2600 South First Street
Springfield, Illinois 62794-9265

© *1992 by* CHARLES C THOMAS • PUBLISHER
ISBN 0-398-05802-4 (cloth)
ISBN 0-398-06137-8 (paper)
Library of Congress Catalog Card Number: 92-404

With THOMAS BOOKS *careful attention is given to all details of manufacturing
and design. It is the Publisher's desire to present books that are satisfactory as to
their physical qualities and artistic possibilities and appropriate for their particular
use.* THOMAS BOOKS *will be true to those laws of quality that assure a good
name and good will.*

Printed in the United States of America
SC-R-3

Library of Congress Cataloging-in-Publication Data

Fryrear, Jerry L.
  Photo art therapy : a Jungian perspective / by Jerry L. Fryrear
and Irene E. Corbit ; with a foreword by Shaun McNiff.
    p.   cm.
  Includes bibliographical references and index.
  ISBN 0398-05802-4.— ISBN 0-398-06137-8 (pbk.)
  1. Photograph in psychotherapy. 2. Art therapy. 3. Jung, C. G.
(Carl Gustav), 1875–1961. I. Corbit, Irene E. II. Title.
  [DNLM: 1. Art Therapy. 2. Jungian Theory. 3. Photography.
WM450.5.P5 F948p]
RC489.P56F78   1992
616.89'1656—dc20
DNLM/DLC
for Library of Congress   92-404
                                                                          CIP

FOREWORD

P*hoto Art Therapy: A Jungian Perspective* illuminates and guides the reader through new possibilities for art therapy practice, approached by Jerry Fryrear and Irene Corbit as a creative interaction with different artistic media and therapeutic methods. Although the book is based on Jungian theory and practice, the authors assiduously explore cooperation with other therapeutic perspectives, all of which are in keeping with Jung's belief in transcendent universals and multifaceted therapeutic practices. A spirit of collaboration permeates every aspect of the coauthored book which not only demonstrates innovative ways of combining artistic media, but allows clients to articulate the inner workings of the therapeutic process through an engaging series of dialogues and narrations. The book establishes a twofold landmark in elucidating art therapy's close and vital connections to both photography and the discipline of Jungian psychotherapy.

Notwithstanding the pioneering contributions of art therapists recognized by the authors (Robert Wolf and Judy Weiser), "phototherapy" and "videotherapy" have generally grown in a parallel relationship to the art therapy profession. In addition to early literature on the therapeutic use of photography (Cornelison and Arsenian, 1960) and videotape (Alger and Hogan, 1967) being published outside the art therapy context, there was a reluctance by many art therapists to embrace these technologies. During the 1970s outspoken art therapists argued that the hegemony of drawing, painting, and modeling with clay should be maintained rather than open to the range of current activities within the visual arts community.

Throughout this period, Jerry Fryrear was experimenting with multi-disciplinary cooperation among the arts which led to his book *The Arts in Therapy,* written with Bob Fleshman in 1981. Fryrear was guided by the historical observation that the arts have always been intimately related, often inseparable, and "prone to a continual effort to recombine, a tendency especially noticeable in modern art." Opposition to the introduction of photography and videotape to art therapy was correctly attuned to the fact that these technologies naturally include drama, movement, and the presentation of the body and thus cross the boundaries of narrow specialization.

After *The Arts in Therapy*, which included a chapter on media arts (videotape, photography, audiotape, and film), Fryrear coedited definitive publications on both phototherapy (1983) and videotherapy (1981). These books confirm how one of our most intelligent advocates of cooperation across the artistic spectrum, can also make authoritative studies of a particular phenomenon, thus demonstrating how comparative study furthers the individuation of a discipline. *Photo Art Therapy* has emerged from this series of books and it completes the process, showing how concentration on a specific technology, instant photography, not only reaches out to other aspects of the visual arts, but includes additional art forms and a treasury of therapeutic possibilities. Coauthorship with Irene Corbit has resulted in a poetic and intimate book focused on therapy as a soulful dialogue between people and the figures of imagination.

Rather than creating yet another creative arts therapy specialization as an offspring from the union of art therapy and phototherapy, Fryrear and Corbit show how art therapy can expand its scope without threatening the integrity of the discipline. They describe how instant photographs invite the participation of other visual arts activities (drawing, painting, collage, *etc.*) when the images are mounted on poster paper or assembled into sculptural figures. Taking pictures of clients also leads to art therapy innovations such as the engagement of the body in "posing" for pictures. The authors' use of instant photographs is in keeping with the photo and videotherapy tradition of "self-image confrontation." However, in contrast to the conventional methods, they actively involve clients in constructing the image and posing for photographs by imagining feeling states and moods through the body. Although this aspect of the experience might be considered secondary to many art therapists, a therapist concentrating on the body and doing the same exercises, will see them as primary. The emphasis on posing suggests a therapy where mind responds to the body's expression of imagery. I have had similar experiences with the presentation of the body as visual image while doing performance art within my art therapy studios.

There is a kinetic orientation to the use of "still" photographs by

Fryrear and Corbit. Their methods involve shifts in body position in correspondence to changing emotions. The reverse is also encouraged by shifting positions and then articulating how changes in the body's pose affect feelings. Photographs externalize these body sensations and establish the basis for further internalization through reflection on the images. Yet another transformation occurs when the photos are arranged on a poster where the artist is free to alter the images, determine how they will be placed on the surface, etc. The authors cite Aaron Beck's "cognitive" therapy as a model for changing habitual imagery, and within the Jungian tradition, James Hillman has similarly encouraged us to change our stories and the fictions according to which we organize our lives. As the images change, we change in correspondence to them. The basis of therapy is the creative action of change, described by Fryrear and Corbit as "visual transitions." They report how subtle changes in actions can stimulate major transformations in a person's life and this is in keeping with Jung's belief that "the savior is either the insignificant thing itself or else arises out of it."

The "self-portrait box" which is used to explore "persona," exemplifies the book's creative explorations. A photograph of an aspect of the artist's persona is attached to each of the six exterior sides of the box and these are accompanied by six "inside" images of private qualities. The process implicitly questions the existence of a single persona and encourages articulation of the many faces that we show, and do not show, to the world. The image of the box with its qualities of containment and its inner sanctum, is useful to those of us who limit artistic expression to two-dimensional surfaces. The simple form of the box combines picture making and sculpture while evoking the work of Joseph Cornell and other links to art.

I enjoyed the authors' reflections upon Jungian theory which appear throughout the book. Jung believed that imagination is the primary faculty of transformation and he encouraged expression of inner states in pictorial form in order to "bring them closer to the patient's under-standing." He tried to stay in close contact with images and avoid "every attempt that the dreamer makes to break away from it." His work still remains an unacknowledged foundation of art therapy practice and this book will help the art therapy community to see that a depth psychology of images cannot overlook Jung.

Irene Corbit's use of "active imagination" in art therapy shows how in-depth psychotherapy naturally involves varied modes of expression and alternatives to ego's habitual speech. Awareness is expanded and welcomes the contributions of expressions that were previously outside the person's consciousness. Sensitivity and safety are furthered by staying in contact with the image which provides the frame for the purposeful and spontaneous movements of psyche which tells its own story.

Trust in psyche's movement within the frame of an image is illustrated by Harry's dream work in Chapter 6. His long walk through sticky mud and chicken dung carrying a plank is one of the most engaging therapeutic dialogues I have ever read. Patient and therapist enter the context of the dream and stay with its qualities through both reflection on images and active imagination, affirming the mystery of the dream and furthering its articulation. The outcome did not solve a puzzle or decipher a hidden cause but seemed to fulfill Jung's desire for the redramatization of the world. He said that when we try to intellectually explain psychic images, "the bird is flown." The dialogue with Harry demonstrates how therapy helps us to imagine our expressions further, more deeply and personally, and within the discipline of an artistic inquiry.

Although photos are the physical forms through which this book individuates itself and contributes to both art and Jungian therapies, they can also be imagined as the universal "widgit," which manifests itself in an unlimited spectrum of physical forms. I urge readers to experience the archetypal forces embodied by the photographs while also keeping a wary eye on the tendency to make any artistic process, such as photographic collage or playing with figures in sand, into a fixity. When a particular method of creation is turned into a school unto itself, it arrests related movements, spin-offs, formal transformations, and unexpected arrivals.

Archetypal forces depend upon the physical forms of the arts in order to manifest themselves in the world, and the arts similarly need the invisible agents of imagination. The Jungian declaration that "image is psyche" suggests an archetypal mainstream entering consciousness through the continuous and surprising movements of imagination as it makes new images.

Photo Art Therapy: A Jungian Perspective offers an exemplary inquiry into one of the myriad channels through which art therapy can be practiced as a discipline of archetypal knowing. Jerry Fryrear and Irene Corbit have worked together to pioneer the art therapy profession in Texas with an open eye on the world. This book invites a wider audience to witness and participate in their creative interaction and I am grateful to have the opportunity to reflect upon the legacy that will surely grow from its pages.

SHAUN McNIFF
Professor
Lesley College Graduate School
Cambridge, Massachusetts

INTRODUCTION

O ur purpose in the present book is to strike a balance between a scholarly treatise about the use of instant photographs and other art media in therapy, and a practical "how to" book with many suggested applications. We hope we have succeeded.

The new technologies have found their places in business, medicine, education, religion, and, recently, in psychotherapy. However, there seems to be a great reluctance on the part of psychotherapists to embrace technology. The field of psychotherapy conjures up images of the Freudian couch and Breuer and Freud's "talking cure" (1895). The client talks and the psychotherapist listens. Other variations of psychotherapy place great emphasis on the relationship between the client and therapist and on personal attributes of the therapist such as warmth and genuineness (see, e.g., Rogers, 1951). As a result of this nearly century-old tradition, many psychotherapists think of themselves as the instrument, the tool, of therapy and are reluctant to admit other, more technical or external tools into the therapy session. One major exception has been biofeedback equipment and the use of audio recorders in relaxation training and guided imagery. Another major exception is the arena of the expressive therapies, where therapists are quick to use art and music media. Very recently, video cameras and photography (in our case, instant photographs) have added new dimensions to the field.

Group and individual therapy sessions can be videotaped for later examination by group members and their therapist (see, e.g., Berger, 1978; Fryrear and Fleshman, 1981; Heilveil, 1983). Photographs can be used to review childhood memories, to confront oneself, and to ease transitions (see Krauss and Fryrear, 1983). Instant photography can allow clients to explore feelings and capture personal images through assumed poses. One pioneer, in particular, has influenced our work. Robert Wolf began using instant photography with children and adolescents many years ago (see Wolf, 1976, 1978, 1983). Working with learning disabled children, antisocial children, and acting-out adolescents, Wolf found instant photography to be helpful in engaging these difficult clients in the therapeutic process. Many of his techniques and ideas inspired our own. The transitional movement work by Houston dance therapist Wynelle Delaney has influenced our thinking, as has other work by people mentioned throughout the book. Interwoven throughout, the concepts of Carl Gustav Jung provide the theoretical thread that holds it all together.

Our work together, using photography combined with other media, began in the early 1980s when we explored the vitality of the expressive arts therapies in group sessions. At that time we led a workshop called "Integrating ancient healing rites and modern technology" in which photography, video, drama, masks, and the arts were used to bring past and present healing methods into force. Since then, we have refined our techniques and added many new methods. Most of the exercises and assignments in this book have come about to fit a specific need for an individual therapy client, a group, or a workshop. They have incubated and birthed as a result of our many therapy experiences and playful brainstorming sessions.

In these pages the reader will find a discussion of art therapy, with emphasis on instant photographs. The invention of instant photography by Edwin Land in 1948 and the modern technology of Polaroid® 600 cameras and film have made it possible to use photos that are taken in therapy, of or by the client, during that same therapy session. From point and shoot to developed color print takes one minute, quicker than drawing or painting a picture. One snapshot costs less than a dollar, certainly not prohibitively expensive. Furthermore, people seem able and willing to take photographs, whereas they may not feel as able to draw or to be "artistic." The photos give a practical and realistic starting place for the creation of works of art, following instructions that are designed to be therapeutic.

For the most part, we approach the scholarly part of the book from the theoretical perspective of C. G. Jung. Of all the great theorists, Jung encouraged multimodal approaches to therapy, and especially mentioned creative and artistic therapies. He did not specifically promote photography, but we like to think that oversight was largely due to the bulky, expensive and impractical photographic technology of his time. Wherever possible and relevant, we shall refer to Jung's writings in the chapters that follow.

By way of introduction, let us quote Jung regarding art therapy. Jung wrote these words in 1916, in a manuscript that remained unpublished until 1958:

> The emotional disturbance can also be dealt with in another way, not by clarifying it intellectually but by giving it visible shape. Patients who possess some talent for drawing or painting can give expression to their mood by means of a picture. It is not important for the picture to be technically or aesthetically satisfying, but merely for the fantasy to have free play and for the whole thing to be done as well as possible . . . a product is created which is influenced by both conscious and unconscious, embodying the striving of the unconscious for the light and the striving of the conscious for substance (Collected Works, Vol. 8, pp. 78–79).

We firmly agree with Jung about giving an emotional disturbance "visible shape." Further, we would say that many, if not most of the issues that come up in psychotherapy can be dealt with better if they have visible shape. Not only disturbances, but moods, relationships, memories, fantasies, anxieties, frustrations, worries, and goals often have no concrete referents. It is much easier for people to confront, discuss, change, and otherwise deal with a concrete referent than an abstract idea. By giving the abstract a "visible shape" the client creates a referent that is quite tangible. It has shape, color, and size and can be directly confronted, discussed, and visibly altered. With a photograph, a client can create a body pose that is a visible shape for an emotion or memory, and can confront, discuss, and alter the photograph in ways that can ultimately and obviously be therapeutic.

We do not believe that patients (or clients as we prefer to call people who seek help) need much artistic ability. It takes very little artistic ability or creativity to pose for a picture, or to cut out and mount a photograph. Artistic ability or training is definitely not a requisite for photo art therapy. A therapy client made this statement: "One unique thing about photographs is the freedom they gave me to not have to worry about not being able to draw! A nonartistic person can take adequate photos; therefore, this technique gave me permission to go for it and not worry about how I would stand up against the work of others."

We do agree emphatically with Jung that the picture need not be technically or aesthetically satisfying. Art therapy departs from art in that the emphasis in art therapy is on the therapy, not the aesthetics. It is a matter of encouraging clients to value the process as an authentic expression, not as some product that will be judged for its artistic expertise. The final artistic product is valuable for therapeutic reasons, and rarely for aesthetic ones. Clients are sometimes embarrassed or frustrated by the inadequacies of their artistic skills, and need extra encouragement by the therapist, but other clients might eagerly create aesthetically pleasing and strikingly dramatic works of art.

Art, with its many media, allows the "fantasy to have free play" as Jung put it. Photography alone is too restrictive, so we supplement the photographs with a large variety of artistic media. We believe in allowing the fantasy to have free play, and subscribe to the idea that the psyche is complex and must be approached in a diverse fashion. Jung wrote, on another occasion in 1935: "The more deeply we penetrate the nature of the psyche, the more the conviction grows upon us that the diversity, the multi-dimensionality of human nature requires the greatest variety of standpoints and methods in order to satisfy the variety of psychic dispositions" (Collected Works, Vol. 16, p. 9).

More recently, McNiff wrote:

> Perhaps the most distinctive feature of an artistic philosophy of therapy is its orientation to multiplicity. Varied images emerge naturally from the psyche, making it necessary for us to be ready for them with as many sensitivities and resources as possible. Inflexible intellectual perspectives make it hard for images to manifest themselves and make it even more difficult for them to be experienced and known by those who work within environments that are not equipped to engage them. . . . The psyche expresses itself in a variety of forms. Individual expressive styles differ, and more than one expressive modality may be useful (1987, pp. 260–261).

One of our clients stated, "With the added paper, glitter, boxes and so on, the photos come to life; all of the 'extras' help define the exercise in a personalized manner." Another group member wrote, "Unequivocally, I experienced a therapeutic efficacy when the art materials were combined with the photos. The combination was marvelously succinct yet facilitated a great deal of conscious and unconscious processing. It amazed me how the art materials that I chose added to the confronting, emotional impact that I thought, at first, was sufficient with the photos alone. In addition, upon observing art products by other group members, it became increasingly apparent how each of us uniquely sought to resolve each issue with colors, shapes, various sizes, and materials that served to direct each of us to explore how we felt about what we did, the feelings our projects stirred in us, and how the integration of art materials and photos together serve to answer profound questions."

In our photo art therapy work we provide clients with instant cameras and film, marking pens, paint and paint brushes, colored yarn, magazines, construction paper, tissue paper, poster board, crayons, scissors, glue, sequins, feathers, glitter, ribbon and whatever else we might have available.

The photo art therapy activities we have developed are designed to provide structure while allowing for a maximum of "free play." We provide broad outlines and direction, but allow for individual creativity.

It is important to provide a structure that is not completely cognitive in nature. There must be allowances for the creation of a product that is "influenced by both conscious and unconscious, embodying the striving of the unconscious for the light and the striving of the conscious for substance." Art therapy, if structured properly, allows for the emergence of unconscious fantasies of which the client may be only dimly aware, if at all. To quote Jung once more: "Critical attention must be eliminated. Visual types should concentrate on the expectation that an inner image will be produced. As a rule such a fantasy-picture will actually appear" (Collected Works, Vol. 8, p. 83). In our work, we encourage clients to play with the art materials, to pursue their first inclinations, to avoid thinking or planning too much. Certain shapes and colors demand to be used in the art work, and if a client is not too cognitive, too intellectual, the fantasy has free play and there is in fact an interplay of conscious and unconscious psychic forces.

The combination of art and photography facilitates this interplay of conscious and unconscious forces. Lambert (1988) remarked, "Art and photography approach the self from two different directions. Art draws first upon the unconscious bringing to the surface that which had been sublimated and frequently unknown to the self. Photography begins with an image outside of the self (objective data as well as a rich source of symbolic data.) The external image can then be generalized and integrated with the internal self. Therefore, I see art and photography complementing each other." In our work, we usually ask that people compose the photographs before actually taking the picture or having it taken of them. Therefore, the resulting image is a portrayal of a conscious, prior concept. Even when people take "snap" shots, no doubt there is some conceptualization before the shot is snapped. After the photograph develops, we then add the subsequent step of artistic augmentation of the photograph with a variety of art media. This second step, the art augmentation or decoration, is not as clearly conceived beforehand. Most people simply let the art proceed without a clear plan. Furthermore, most people report that they become absorbed in the art work, and enter a kind of trance while they are using the materials. This second step, adding the art to the photograph, may help the client come in contact with feelings, thoughts and memories that are not readily accessable to active, conscious thought. In other words, the photographic part of the assignment is conscious and intentional. The artistic part of the assignment is more unconscious and automatic.

A pervasive theme in Jung's writings is the tension of opposites. With regard to conscious and unconscious, Jung writes over and over again that the conscious psyche compensates for the unconscious and vice versa. The compensatory nature of the psyche makes it inevitable that tension will exist in the individual. The person overcomes that tension of opposites by the transcendent function. That is, by becoming more than simply a bundle of tension. The transcendent function depends on the process of individuation, whereby a person becomes all he or she can be. Jung wrote:

> The transcendent function does not proceed without aim and purpose, but leads to the revelation of the essential man. It is in the first place a purely natural process, which may in some cases pursue its course without the knowledge or assistance of the individual, and can sometimes forcibly accomplish itself in the face of opposition. The meaning and purpose of the process is the realization, in all its aspects, of the personality originally hidden away in the embryonic germ-plasm; the production and unfolding of the original, potential wholeness. The symbols used by the unconscious to this end are the same as those which mankind has always used to express wholeness, completeness and perfection: symbols, as a rule, of the quaternity and the circle. For these reasons I have termed this the *individuation process* (Collected Works, Vol 7, p. 110).

The individuation process is possible only with increasing knowledge of one's personality. The particular combination of photographs and artwork, as we have discussed above, is a powerful method for assisting a person in the quest for personal knowledge and transcending the tension of opposites.

The present book is divided into four sections: *Self-understanding, Alleviating Distress and Symptoms, Group Therapy,* and *Discussion.* Where possible and practical, we reproduce photo art therapy work done by clients as illustrations of the concepts.

The first section contains six chapters that have to do with understanding oneself in the quest for individuation. Chapter 1 is a discussion of photo art therapy assignments that aid in understanding oneself in relation to the natural world. Chapter 2 contains methods for understanding one's relationships to other people. Chapter 3 gives instructions and methods for exploring the "persona," or that personality that we project onto others. Chapter 4 concerns the "shadow," that part of the personality that is not easily acknowledged or valued. Chapter 5 is a discussion of photo art therapy and archetypes, particularly with reference to folk tales and fairy tales. Chapter 6 concludes the first section of the book with a photo art therapy approach to dreams and active imagination.

Section Two contains specific suggestions for direct therapy of psychological symptoms such as anxiety, depression, and phobias, with illustrated examples. Chapter 7 has to do with fears, with special reference to children, including work with sandplay combined with photographs. Chapter 8 addresses the use of photo art therapy in resolving intrapersonal conflict. Chapter 9 is the use of photo art therapy in dealing with apathy, indecision, and depression. Chapter 10 is a case study of an adult survivor of childhood abuse who used the photo art therapy methods to nurture that hurt child within and to overcome the effects of the abuse.

In Section Three we have three chapters on group therapy. Chapter 11, "The Visual Transitions Group," is a description of a photo art therapy group technique developed by the authors that is multimodal in nature, incorporating art, photography, video, movement, and verbal discussion. Chapters 12 and 13 address the common problems in group therapy of developing group cohesion and breathing new life into a "stuck" group.

Section Four consists of two chapters only. Chapter 14 is primarily a discussion of the ethics of confidentiality, and practical matters, such as art materials, with some brief descriptions of photo or video art programs that are new, not completely developed, or that do not fit conceptually within any other chapter. Chapter 15 is a brief summary of the book. We conclude the book with a list of references.

To avoid sexist language and the awkward he/she, herself/himself construction, we arbitrarily use feminine pronouns in some passages and masculine ones in others. The identities of clients are disguised and all art reproductions of clients are reprinted with permission.

ACKNOWLEDGMENTS

Several people helped with this book at various stages. Ingrid Bender provided some material. Jan Perry, Librarian at the Houston C. G. Jung Educational Center, was a source for references. Dr. May Paulissen and Dr. David Vest read early versions of the manuscript and gave us valuable suggestions. Barbara Butler typed several chapters. We especially want to thank the people who graciously allowed us to reproduce their artwork and comments about themselves.

CONTENTS

PHOTO ART THERAPY

SECTION ONE
SELF–UNDERSTANDING

The self is a central concept in all personality theories and in every-day life. We say a person is selfish, we talk about self-concept, self-esteem, self-motivated, self-made, myself, herself, self-realization, self-actualization, and on and on. Talking about "self" is easy. Defining "self" is not so easy. At one point, Jung described self this way:

> Conscious and unconscious are not necessarily in opposition to one another, but complement one another to form a totality, which is the *self.* According to this definition the self is a quantity that is superordinate to the conscious ego. It embraces not only the conscious but also the unconscious psyche, and is therefore, so to speak, a personality which we *also* are ... It transcends our powers of imagination to form a clear picture of what we are as a self, for in this operation the part would have to comprehend the whole. There is little hope of our ever being able to reach even approximate consciousness of the self, since however much we may make conscious there will always exist an indeterminate amount of unconscious material which belongs to the totality of the self. Hence the self will always remain a superordinate quantity (Collected Works, Vol. 7, p. 175).

If we can't ever really understand ourselves, why try? Is self-understanding or self-knowledge worth the effort? Jung (Collected Works, Vol. 7) emphasized that self-knowledge, and the action that follows that knowledge, allow one to free oneself from the tyranny of the ego. Instead of being bound by the egotistical world of personal wishes, hopes, and fears, one can be freer to participate in the larger world of more objective interests.

Clearly, Jung felt that self-knowledge is a good thing. We agree wholeheartedly and have designed photo art therapy activities with self-knowledge as the goal. In this first section, we give details of six different approaches to self-knowledge. Chapter 1 addresses the question of self as it relates to the natural world. Chapter 2 is concerned more with oneself in relation to other people. Chapter 3 has to do with the persona, that part of our personality that we groom for presentation to the world. Chapter 4 delves into the dark side of the personality, the dimly perceived shadow side. Chapter 5 looks at the broader view of archetypes. Chapter 6 is a discussion of understanding the self through dreams and active imagination. These concepts will be described and discussed more fully at the beginning of each of the chapters. In each chapter we reproduce artwork done by clients in their attempts at self-understanding, and their comments about the work.

Chapter 1

RELATING TO NATURE

You jolt awake to a strident alarm clock in a climate-controlled building whose windows are permanently sealed. You bathe in preheated water, eat processed breakfast food, ride in an elevator to the enclosed parking garage. Encased in a climate-controlled automobile, you enter the concrete freeway teeming with other encased people, all alone in their automobiles, protected from the elements and each other. Exiting the freeway, you enter another enclosed parking garage and take another elevator to a climate-controlled office, where you spend the day in artificial light. At 5:00 P.M. you reverse the process.

Contrast this scenario with the next one:

You awaken with the dawn, stretch luxuriously, sit up and put your feet on the floor. Finding your slippers, you wander out to the kitchen and make a pot of coffee. With your steaming coffee cup in hand, you quietly walk out onto the porch to watch the sun come up over the trees. Out in the meadow, the mist hangs in low patches just above the ground. At the edge of the trees in the meadow, six does and two fawns graze on the misty grass. You can just see the twitching ears of the young fawns above the mist, which comes up to their mothers' knees. The does' heads disappear momentarily as they stretch down to graze, then emerge as they raise back up, ever alert for predators. You can't see him, but you suspect that a buck is acting as sentinel at the fringe of the trees.

As the sun gradually lights up the meadow and burns off the mist, the colors turn from gray to pink and the deer drift out of sight into the cover of the forest. You hear a mockingbird on the highest limb in the live oak tree at the corner of the house, and two scarlet cardinals chirp as their vivid colors stand out against the deep green of the holly bush at the end of the porch. Overhead a red-shouldered hawk cruises the meadow, looking for a careless mouse for breakfast. Her mate sits motionless on a dead limb near the top of a tree at the edge of the forest. Later you will see them hunting together.

It is now full daylight and you refill your coffee cup and return to the porch where you sit on the steps. A rustling in the grass next to the oak tree gets your attention and you notice a gray squirrel out early burying acorns for the future. Most of them he will forget about and some will sprout to mark the beginnings of new oak trees. Your gaze is drawn upward toward the top of the oak tree outlined against the blue sky, where you see the squirrel's nest in a fork of a limb high out of reach of danger. In February there were baby squirrels there; perhaps this squirrel digging now so industriously in the grass was born in that very nest.

As you immerse yourself in the early morning sights and smells, you become more attuned to the small creatures that share your world. A spider waits in her dew-sparkled web, gnats' miniature wings glisten in the sun, a butterfly folds and unfolds her wings, then flies away in her erratic wanderings. You become aware that you are one among millions, billions of living creatures. Earthworms tunnel blindly beneath your feet. Hordes of caterpillars chomp on leaves. Still smaller creatures eat and are eaten, reproduce and die in the endless cycle of nature.

With a clarity that seems to equal the morning sun, you *know* that you are one with nature. All life is interdependent and you are part of it. Without the plants and animals you would not exist any more than they. The vast resources of the earth are not there for you to use and discard, but to use and renew. With a feeling of contentment mixed with awe and humility, you go back inside to get ready for the rest of the day.

One big problem of our time is the urge to control and use nature rather than be a part of it. We dam rivers, cut trees, kill animals, build elaborate protection from the natural elements. At the same time, we want to return to nature, to garden, to go camping, hiking, boating, skiing. This basic ambivalence in our relationship to nature is the theme for this chapter. The exercises we have developed are designed to help clients better understand their relationship to nature. An understanding of one's relationship to nature, furthermore, leads to an understanding of one's own psyche. Jung recognized that, in our quest for conscious reason and understanding, we risk alienating ourselves from the natural world:

Analytical psychology is a reaction against the exaggerated rationalization of consciousness which, seeking to control nature, isolates itself from her and so robs man of his own natural history. He finds himself transplanted into a limited present, consisting of the short span between birth and death. The limitation creates a feeling that he is a haphazard creature without meaning, and it is this feeling that prevents him from living his life with the intensity it demands if it is to be enjoyed to the full. Life becomes stale and is no longer the exponent of the complete man. That is why so much unlived life falls into the unconscious. People live as though they are walking in shoes too small for them. That quality of eternity which is so characteristic of the life of primitive man is entirely lacking. Hemmed round by rationalistic walls, we are cut off from the eternity of nature. Analytical psychology seeks to break through these walls by digging up again the fantasy-images of the unconscious which our rationalism has rejected. These images lie beyond the walls; they are part of the nature *in us,* which apparently lies buried in our past and against which we have barricaded ourselves behind the walls of reason. Analytical psychology tries to resolve the resultant conflict not by going "back to nature" with Rousseau, but by holding on to the level of reason we have successfully reached, and by enriching consciousness with a knowledge of man's psychic foundations (Collected Works, Vol. 8, pp. 380–381).

In our photo art therapy assignments we do not ask, "What is nature?" or "What can I do about nature?" Rather we ask, "Who am I in relation to nature?" This question does not refute our present level of reason, but at the same time it requires that we "dig up the fantasy-images of the unconscious which our rationalization has rejected." These fantasy-images become visible shapes in the form of photographs and other art media on the background of poster board. By examining our relationship to nature, we come to appreciate the timelessness of natural rhythms and our place in the natural world.

The natural world is everywhere and everything that can be seen or touched. By natural, then, we mean that which is not purely spiritual or fanciful. However, the natural world is symbolic of the spiritual and psychological. In mythology, for example, we see myriad examples of natural symbols for supernatural fantasies. Furthermore, these mythological symbols are in turn symbols that reflect psychic processes. "All of the mythologized processes of nature, such as summer and winter, the phases of the moon, the rainy seasons, and so forth, are in no sense allegories of these objective occurrences; rather they are symbolic expressions of the inner, unconscious drama of the psyche which becomes accessible to man's consciousness by way of projection—that is, mirrored in the events of nature" (Jung, Collected Works, Vol. 9, Pt. 1, page 6).

By coming to know our relationship to nature, we not only feel more "in tune with" nature and appreciative of our natural history, but we also come to know more about our own psyches through the age-old symbols of nature itself. The sky through the ages has become symbolic of the spiritual. Plants and animals can symbolize life itself and the reproduction process. Some animals are symbolic of different emotions for many people. The rabbit is fearful. The lion is confident and proud. The dog is friendly. Water reflects the depths of the psyche. Earth is the nurturing medium for all life.

Nature Activity

For the "Who am I in relation to nature" activity, we provide clients with poster board, camera and film, scissors, glue, and assorted art materials. We ask the clients to think of themselves in relation to the earth, the sky, animals, plants and water, and to imagine how one could pose to depict these five relationships. It is not necessary to compose the perfect photograph with the perfect natural background, because with the art supplies one can draw in animals, mountains, trees or anything else. One can also cut out pictures from magazines to add to the artistic composition. We do, however, encourage people to pose for the photographs outdoors so that they can be more attentive to nature.

When the client has decided on a pose, the therapist or other therapy group member takes the snapshot. Altogether, there will be five such snapshots for each person.

After the client has the five snapshots, the therapist asks the client to think about how one could compose the five photographs on a piece of poster board to represent a self-portrait in relation to nature. The images can be cut out from the frames and the background of the poster board can be embellished with the other media, such as oil pastels, tissue paper, construction paper, marking pens, ribbons, and yarn. Many people also gather leaves, grass, bark, feathers and other natural objects and add them to the art work.

We set the mood by encouraging people to approach this assignment with a playful and excited attitude. As with all of the exercises in this book, there is no right or wrong way to do the work. Also, it does not matter if the final product is artistic. We ask people to trust their innate creativity and to "go with" whatever seems to feel "right." People find that, if they move the materials around on the poster board, trying out different shapes, colors, and objects, a visible shape will emerge that seems correct. Some people prefer to use five different poster boards, and to prepare the five poses separately.

After the poster is prepared, we simply ask the client to talk about the artwork. If we are working with a group, we usually have people pair off and talk to each other first, then to the group as a whole. We caution group members to listen uncritically, without trying to analyze or criticize. Rather than analyze the art work, we prefer to allow the client to talk about the work as much as possible, and to make as many associations as possible. The therapist may ask leading questions or make comments such as, "Tell me about that particular shape," or, "I notice that there is a connection between this photograph and the green circle."

As people talk about their artwork, they frequently remark that they wish they had done some part differently. We encourage people to change the work in whatever way they want to, adding new photographs, changing colors or shapes, or whatever they wish. As the fantasy changes, the image changes. It is the process that is important, not the product.

Bonnie

In 1987, four years ago, Bonnie was a participant in a weekend intensive workshop at a beach house on Galveston Island. There were eight participants and the two leaders, Irene E. Corbit and Jerry L. Fryrear. In addition to assigning a number of other art therapy projects that weekend, we asked the participants to prepare three posters representing "Who am I in relation to nature?" Because of time constraints, we only assigned "Who am I in relation to air," "Who am I in relation to water," and "Who am I in relation to the earth."

At that time, Bonnie's father was seriously ill with a terminal disease. In her mind, he was already gone, and she was grieving for him. Outwardly, Bonnie did not show her grief. She was somewhat haughty and seemed unconcerned about other people. Perhaps because of her apparent aloofness, at one point during the weekend, some of the other group members verbally attacked her. When they did, others came to her defense. It was her artwork that weekend that penetrated to the real motives of her actions, showing her grief in a most obvious way. Her drawings revealed the use of mostly black and gray, and her productions were minimal. As one illustration, we reproduce here her poster depicting "Who am I in relation to water." The poster shows Bonnie kneeling in a pensive posture at the edge of the surf. On either side of her photograph, she drew three large gray columns, the three on the right and the three on the left connected by arching gray lines drawn over and through her photograph. Below her photograph and the columns are three wavy gray lines of water.

In response to a query, Bonnie wrote about the poster, "Grief. My family was seven, now six. The center rays are the energy from my father. They surround me even though he is gone."

We contacted Bonnie in August, 1991, regarding the use of her artwork for this book, and she graciously agreed to an interview about the work. Here is what she said:

> Who am I in relationship to water (poster reproduced above). In 1987, I was in the grief process for my father. Now, in 1991, I find myself again in the grief process—this time for a close friend who is dying of cancer. As I look at this picture many of the same feelings surface. The water represents the timelessness

Figure 1-1. Bonnie's poster, "Who Am I in Relationship to Water?"

of the life process and gives me a sense of peace. Using the strength of my family I have been able to care for my friend in a loving way and to release him to his dying process. Without the energy I feel from this source, I would have found this process much more painful. Again I have been able to go inward and look at my own mortality and make new decisions about my life.

Who am I in relationship to air (poster not shown). This picture shows a small airplane flying over the beach with blue and yellow lines connecting plane to sun. In the lower right corner is a design showing the freedom of color and line and containing the spiral of life. Today the feelings from this picture remain very much the same. I still use flying to gain perspective when my life gets complicated. To be creative within the design is both rewarding and stimulating when the design is of my making, not someone else's. My life for the last four years has been rich, complicated, and difficult. I am content with my design.

Who am I in relationship to the earth (poster not shown). In this picture I used beach stones, sticks and shells to make a design in the sand. I drew lines around the design to show the ripples from my father's life never ending. I realize this is true for my friend as well. Even after his death, his influence on my life will shape my response to the future.

As I look at these pictures I created four years ago, I realize my message for today is that death doesn't interrupt love. I believe this exercise will give me the strength I need to assist my dying friend. Thanks.

During the intervening four years, Bonnie has created a great number of collages for her personal therapy. Unlike the poster shown above, her more recent art is rich and complicated, with vivid colors and textures. She, herself, is complicated and rich in personality as we believe she is coming to understand.

Each participant in this nature exercise will approach it differently. In Chapter 10 we print the art work and the remarks made by Judith, a woman who had an abused childhood. Some of that artwork was in response to the Nature assignment. Her work is much more detailed and optimistic than Bonnie's shown here. Indeed, each person who carries out this nature exercise will approach it differently.

As one final example, here are the comments made by Helga (artwork not shown) about her nature poster. Helga's photo art therapy assignment concerning her Shadow is presented in Chapter 4, along with a few details about her life. Helga put all five Nature assignments on the same poster board. She posed for four of the photographs in a small park outside the office, and she posed for one with stuffed toy animals—a mouse and a bear, inside the building. She commented:

This poster represents my relationship to nature. In the top picture you see my relationship to the sky. With arms stretched out, I would like to be one with the sky. I love the sky, especially here in Texas. It always offers something interesting, a drama, a story. Especially fascinating to me is the evening sky with its beautiful, glowing range of colors from yellow, orange to violet and silver gray. When on cold days, I watch the cloud formation, I often think of the song "Who has the most beautiful sheep . . ." At times the clouds look as though they are covered with pink chiffon. If I had enough training to paint these sky pictures, I would produce one sky picture after the other. The sky often has a conciliatory quality. I sometimes have pictures of the war before my eyes when I walked through the city damaged by bombs, and, when right after an air raid the rubble was still smoldering. But the sun shone on the ruins as though nothing had happened, as if she wanted to say, "What are you people doing?" Just like a mockery of nature.

The rainbow. Each person would probably like to have a rainbow in her life. It is symbolic for beauty. I love rainbows like I love the sky. But sometimes people do not have rainbows in their lives and in order to have a rainbow it must first rain. Rain is important for the earth, nature, and people. Symbolically rain probably means something sad in the lives of people. Each person will at some time experience something sad in her life, but it would be much nicer if we did not need to experience this. I could easily do without it.

These pictures depict my relationship to plants. Well, that is a theme without end! In this picture I snuggle up to a tree. I like trees so very much and can occupy much of my time with them. This tree has the foliage of last year and the spring blossoms of this year. Unbelievable!

I love fall with all its beautiful colors, and I like especially the first cool north winds and the winter when it gets cold. One can go for a stroll and come home refreshed. When the trees in a ghostlike manner stretch their bare branches toward the sky, they offer wonderful statues to paint; especially when covered with Spanish moss they resemble some old ghosts.

I make many discoveries in nature and with plants. If only I had more time I would paint many nature scenes. Sometimes a single tree is fascinating to me. Or, to paint a picture of only leaves in their varied forms and colors would be a lot of fun. I always wanted to write a story of the runaway leaves. One day I will do it.

Of course, I cannot imagine nature without flowers. I care for my flowers as though they are my children, and they bloom thankfully. Often I sing a song with this work, "A flower was given to me." I can hardly stand to pull up flowers. Usually I let them grow until they die. Two rosebushes in front of our window are 31 years old and still producing flowers.

The next picture is to show my relationship to the earth. I am lying in the juicy light green grass. The little blades are so tender and soft and it feels as though I am lying on moss. It is very comfortable. The earth includes most everything, for we live on earth. The earth supplies us with everything which we need to live, therefore, the expression "mother earth."

My relationship to the animals is depicted in the picture with the bear and the mouse. I enjoy animals very much and they too are being cared for like my children. We have some chickens, and, before I knew that they like to stand in the rain, we ran outside each time it rained and brought them into the henhouse. After all, I was raised in the city and had to learn that they did not need to be brought inside. Animals are company to me. It is relaxing to watch them. Only when animals become aggressive, do I avoid them. Even when dogs jump up on me for joy, I dislike it. I find mice comical. I especially like young animals.

The last picture denotes my relationship to water. Water is necessary for all life and even for concrete, so that it does not break. I love the ocean which is not far from here and enjoy jumping into the waves. The water of the gulf is as warm as bath water and sometimes it feels as though the waves caress the body. The best thing to do here during the summer is to go swimming.

The dark brown yarn on my poster is to bring some interest into the otherwise monotonous green area of grass. I find many green and brown colors in nature. When I saw the pink and brown yarn I was reminded how, as a child,

I liked the color combination of pink and dark brown. And so I wanted somehow to bring them together in this picture.

Bonnie, Helga and Judith all approached this assignment differently, yet each seemed to come to some sort of resolution or conclusion from the exercises. Our experience has been that the nature assignments do act as reminders of our unseverable relationships with nature.

Chapter 2

RELATING TO OTHERS

It is obvious that human beings are social beings. As a species we gather in family units, businesses and professions, social clubs, communities, towns, cities, states, and nations. In these various social units we relate to each other every day. Each of us comes to an interaction with a basic social orientation that determines the nature and outcome of the interaction. Fundamentally, Jung was in agreement with Alfred Adler that we are basically interested in each other, need each other, and desire to live harmoniously. He also agreed with Adler's concepts of superiority and inferiority and the will to power (see Collected Works, Vol. 7). That is, there is a constant interplay between social interest on the one hand and the striving for superiority or power on the other. When the striving for superiority overrides the need for harmonious relationships, a neurotic or self-defeating life style exists.

To Adler's basic concepts, Jung added his well-known attitudes of extraversion and introversion, attitudes that apply to all of life and especially to our relationships to others. One can be, in one's conscious life, extraverted and outgoing or introverted and shy. These basic orientations of superiority and inferiority, introversion and extraversion, can describe and explain much of one's orientations toward others.

In his complex theory, Jung delved much more deeply into relationships and discussed the archetypes of anima and animus, present in all of us (see Chapter 5 for a more elaborate discussion of archetypes). The anima is the feminine archetype in men and the animus is the masculine archetype in women. Because of these two archetypes, we all unconsciously have automatic knowledge of the opposite gender because we all have both feminine characteristics and masculine characteristics within us. Men identify their egos, or consciousness with masculinity and the corresponding feminine side is unconscious, while women identify themselves consciously as feminine while the masculine side is unconscious.

Sanford (1980) calls the unconscious anima and animus "invisible partners" in a relationship. He writes:

14

All of this has important implications for the relationship between the sexes. Men, identified with their masculinity, typically project their feminine side onto women, and women, identified with their feminine nature, typically project their masculine side onto men. These projected psychic images are the invisible partners in every man-woman relationship, and greatly influence the relationship, for wherever projection occurs the person who carries the projected image is either greatly overvalued or greatly undervalued. In either case, the human reality of the individual who carries a projection for us is obscured by the projected image. This is especially the case with the anima and animus since these archetypes are so numinous. This means that they are charged with psychic energy, so that they tend to grip us emotionally. Consequently these projected images have a magnetic effect on us, and the person who carries a projection will tend to greatly attract or repel us, just as a magnet attracts or repels another metal (p. 13).

In every relationship there are, so to speak, four personalities interacting, the obvious partners and the invisible partners. There is therefore ample room for confusion and contradiction. Furthermore, the anima and animus have both negative and positive qualities, and the projected anima or animus may appear extremely desirable at one moment and suddenly repellant at the next, regardless of what the other person is actually like.

Schutz (1958) added yet another analysis of our social orientations. In addition to the extraversion/introversion and superiority/inferiority dimensions, and the archetypal underpinnings, Schutz suggests that we should consider the three areas of Inclusion, Control, and Affection as the three most important orientations. Further, he amplified his model to reflect the extent to which we desire inclusion, control from others, and affection from others, and the extent to which we want to include others in our activities, to control others, and to show affection toward others. We can readily see that Schutz's model meshes well with both Jung and Adler. A shy, introverted person would not want to be included in other people's activities, nor would she exhibit affection, although she well might desire affection from others. A person who was striving for superiority would want to control others, but might not be interested in affection. The projected anima and animus serve to intensify or distort the desires.

Schutz (1978) developed and published a questionnaire, the Fundamental Interpersonal Relations Orientation-Behavior (FIRO–B) that aids in identifying a person's orientations in the three areas of inclusion, control, and affection. Likewise, the Myers-Briggs Type Indicator (MBTI) is a questionnaire developed from Jungian theory that helps to identify a person's level of introversion or extraversion (Briggs and Myers, 1977). Therapists and clients may find these instruments helpful.

In spite of our continual need for mutually productive and satisfying relations with others, people rarely examine their basic social orientations. In this photo art therapy assignment, the client is asked to do that. To what extent is the client striving for superiority over others, or succumbing to a feeling of inferiority? How introverted or extraverted is the client? To what extent is the client aware of the animus or anima archetypes? How about the areas of inclusion, control, and affection? Does the client want to control others, yet wants no one to control him? Does he desire affection from others but cannot show affection? Is he projecting his own anima to such an extent that it obscures the real other person? It seems obvious to us that a better understanding of one's social orientation is basic to a better relationship with others. Better relationships with others, in turn, leads to more satisfying lives for us all.

Relating to Others Assignment

We call this photo art therapy assignment "Who am I in Relation to Other People?" More specifically, there are three exercises, "Who am I in relation to men," "Who am I in relation to women," and "Who am I in relation to children." Other, still more specific assignments are possible with certain clients, if relevant. As examples, clients might examine their relations to elderly people, students, teachers, black people, white people, or even a spouse or other individual.

The therapist and client have a discussion about the relationship orientations that we have described above. It might be helpful to include the FIRO–B and the MBTI questionnaire results to help the client see the orientations more clearly. Following the discussion, the client is asked to choose one of the three relationships, and decide on a pose or poses that reflect the basic orientation toward that group of people. The therapist, or group partner, takes the snapshots of the client posing.

The photograph images are cut out and mounted on a piece of poster board, and the poster is completed with other art media. Construction paper, colored marking pens, oil pastels, tissue paper, magazine pictures, yarn, and ribbon are helpful additions. The poster is a depiction of the assignment "Who am I in relation to men (or women, or children)?"

Processing

In individual therapy, the therapist uses the poster board as a referent and focus of the therapy. In groups, the photography partners first share their poster boards with each other, giving as much detail as comfortable, then sharing with the larger group. In groups especially, and to a lesser extent with the therapist, the sharing phase is somewhat awkward because the partner or therapist is a member of one of the groups of people being discussed. If the client is examining his relationship to women, and the therapist or group partner is a woman, then the therapist or partner is an object of the examination. To an extent the therapist, and more likely the group partner, will take whatever the client says somewhat personally. Therapists and group members must take special pains to avoid becoming defensive.

As an illustration, we shall reproduce the artwork done by "James" in response to the activity "Who am I in relationship to other men?" The therapy session is transcribed verbatim below and shows how the artwork can become the focal point for the verbal part of the therapy. The photography and artwork were done in one session, and the verbal processing a week later. The illustration given here is one of several photo art therapy sessions in which James participated. During the initial discussion of relationships, James found the everyday language of Schutz to be quite helpful in deciding how to proceed with the photographs and the art. The therapist is Jerry Fryrear.

James

James is a 40-year-old divorced father who has custody of his two young children. He entered into therapy originally in order to understand his emotions more clearly and to gain control over his sometimes frightening anger. He approached the therapy assignments very seriously. He gave all of the photography, art work and verbal processing his undivided and careful attention.

The "Who am I in relation to men" poster includes three photographs of James, three "negatives" of the photographs, and three drawings made on colored construction paper. The three photographs are mounted on differently colored backgrounds of construction paper. A verbatim transcript of the therapy session follows. The therapist is Jerry L. Fryrear. The therapist's comments are in italics.

> *James:* The pictures I took of myself are myself, and the pictures that I drew are other men.

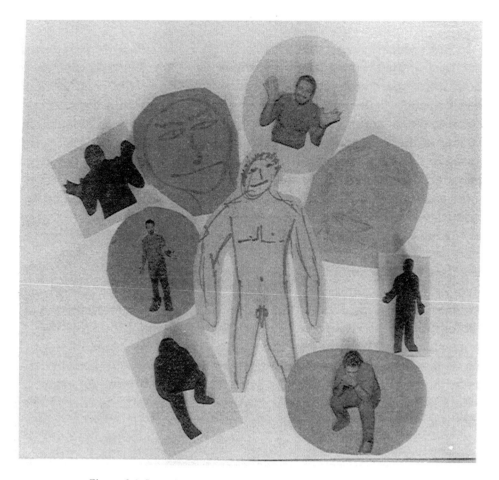

Figure 2-1. James's poster, "Who am I in Relationship to Men?"

Are those specific men or men in general?
James: I wasn't thinking of anybody, just other males. But they are different aspects of other males. These are different parts of me as I want other people to see me (pointing to the photographs of himself). These negatives that I took off the back of my pictures are some aspects of myself that I am not sure of, a gray area.
Start with the three photographs, and explain those.
James: This is me in my approach relationship to other males (lower right photo), cautious, guarded, tense, and apprehensive.

This is me opening up as I progress (left-hand photo), as I get comfortable and show more of myself, to be vulnerable, and to want more from the other person. This (upper right photo) is me as I am able to be with some males that I know. Relaxed, spontaneous, open. It's more my ideal, but it's not able to happen in all cases.

What do you have to know about another man before you can be that way?

James: I'm not sure. I guess that they are similar to me in some ways, inside.

So when you see you have some things in common, some things you share, some values maybe ...

James: Uh huh. We take a few risks together. You know, it can't happen with everybody. But over time, as I see more of them and they see more of me.

And there are some people in your life right now that you can be more open with, and not guarded.

James: Uh huh. Although that sometimes takes time to reach that level.

More time than you would like? Would you like to reach that level quicker?

James: No. I'm finding that there's a time and I am comfortable with it.

You sort of appreciate the fact that you can be reserved and guarded for a period of time.

James: I decided to put these up here (the three black negatives) because there are times in my relationships with other men when I am uncertain and uncomfortable about the me that I am trying to present, the way I want to be seen. I feel that there are certain defenses, that I have certain images that I want to be revealed. It's more of a guarded posture because I am still probing the other person to find out who it's okay to be with.

Have you had experiences where you trusted people too quickly and they didn't treat you well?

James: Yes, I can think of several in particular. Probably I allowed myself to be too vulnerable, and felt betrayed, expected too much from them as far as acceptance. These (the three drawings) are different male personas. No one in particular, that I know of. This (center drawing on yellow construction paper) is the fully-revealed male. It is robust, not hidden, somebody that I wouldn't mind being close to, who's not afraid for me to be close to them and to reveal themselves to me. It corresponds more to this aspect of myself here (upper self-photograph).

Nothing to hide and open.

James: Uh huh, but still more idealized than real. I'm not sure that I have this type of relationship with anybody.

And it's a natural relationship.

James: Uh huh. (long pause)

And the other two drawings?

James: Up here, up here, that I'm getting to know ... (upper left drawing on red construction paper).

That's an actual person?

James: No. There are no specific people here, although I guess I could relate them to specific people. This is males as often I see them to begin with, and it's, uh, they are looking at me like they're trying to check me out, size me up.

Not very friendly looking.

James: No. Squinty eyes to see where you're at.

Judgmental, looks like to me too.

James: There's also a certain quality of trying to discern ... yeah, judgment I guess. And some relationships never get beyond this point.

You stay in a position where they are sizing you up and you are sizing them up too.

James: And that corresponds with this and this (pointing to photo of self in lower right and then photo on left). Sometimes it will fluctuate back and forth to this (left photo) and back to this (lower right photo). Occasionally I get like this (left photo) as I think that I can, that it's safe to, to see if they'll move beyond here (upper left drawing). Mostly it will go back to here (lower right photo) and we will terminate the relationship unless it's a forced relationship like work or school or something.

How do specific people fit into this? One obvious person is of course your father, as one male. Is he a person you can be open with, or do you have to be guarded and wary of him? Is he still alive, by the way?

James: Yes. I can find my relationship with him in each of these pictures.

It's a complicated relationship.

James: There is a bit of this here, still (upper left drawing).

He still looks at you kind of squinty eyed, sizing you up.

James: Not so much. Mostly I see him like this and like this (other two drawings). Occasionally I see my father like this (middle drawing), we're very open and spontaneous with each other. Sometimes I see him like this (right hand drawing on green construction paper) as a person that's becoming, that has, some kind of sensitive qualities and I recognize him and respect him for his limitations that don't meet up to what this ideal would be (pointing to middle drawing). Sometimes I have a standoffish feeling about him, like here (lower right photo). That's been cyclic and not very often, but I end up being very disappointed when that happens. I withdraw for a period of time.

Have you been able to pinpoint what leads up to that, what triggers that?

James: I just know that it's happened in situations where I allow him to be in a position of authority or judgment on me. Then something about the relationship changes. It becomes like I'm the shameful little boy and he's the angry father.

When you start feeling like a little boy, is when ...

James: I feel like he treats me like a little boy at times. I'm not necessarily feeling like a little boy. Sometimes I'm starting to act like an adult and feel like I'm not being accepted as one. There may be a time in there when I assume that role.

I was thinking that this (right-hand drawing) represents a specific person. I just had an image of him in my mind. Probably my best friend in high school who is dead now. He was one of the people that I felt had a special protective love in relationship to me. We regarded and admired each other without too much judgment. Yet we were free to tell each other when we disapproved. We just felt very open.

You had a real natural relationship with him. You didn't feel guarded, like you had to watch yourself.

James: No, I didn't. He died of a congenital heart defect. He lived long beyond what they expected him to, and when he died, it was kind of sad. It was sad when he died, but the funeral was kind of a celebration, like a good send off.

How old were you when he died?

James: It was five years ago. Thirty-five. He was a year older than I was.

So you lost a really close friend.

James: Although we hadn't been close for a few years because he had a family and moved. We kept up the relationship. I guess it was sad because I hadn't seen him for a few years and taken too much a part in his life. He had achieved some successes and stabilized out his family and professional life and I hadn't been too much a part of that.

Did you go to the funeral?

James: Uh huh. (long pause, looking at artwork)

See anything else?

James: I was aware that there was a progression from when I started doing it, even from the time we took the photographs and I did them in this sequence. And it feels like there's something missing here. I know that in my relationships with males that I want to go up here (upper photo) and stay, but I feel uncomfortable here (lower right photo) and know that the relationship won't last long if it doesn't get out of there, if it can't get to here (upper left) and back and forth (upper left to upper right) occasionally. And something else is missing in between those three too.

Some other stage, you mean?

James: Uh huh, yeah. I'm not sure if it's . . . Maybe there's two of them. It seems like there's some anger and withdrawal, like when I feel hurt.

What about the colors? Sometimes colors can represent those emotions. You used blue, red, yellow, and green. Were you thinking at the time about the colors?

James: I wasn't thinking of them in terms of expressing emotions, but I was aware that I wanted some sort of balance of colors and I wanted them to be primary so that I could identify them with something. This yellow here (upper photo background) represents an expansiveness.

And the red?

James: (long pause) I don't know. When I look at this one (left photo background) the red is like warmness, but here (upper left drawing) it's almost like anger or something.

One of the things that you and Nancy (previous therapist) talked about last year was getting in touch with anger. What might be going on is a confusion of emotions. Sometimes it feels like anger, and sometimes it feels more like warmth or something like that.

James: And this (blue lower right photo background) is like isolation but not always in a negative sense. Sometimes it's being withdrawn into myself and feeling secure with it, too. That it's okay to be alone, and sometimes I need to be here too.

One thing that struck me is that you've matched up a drawing with a photograph, using the red and yellow, but not with the blue. Then you went to green for the drawing. Maybe that's what you feel is missing. There's not a match for the blue, the isolation.

James: Of course, my logic when I put it together was that I was using primary colors.

And you wanted to get all of them in there.

James: Uh huh.

When you are isolated, there aren't other people, so a lack of match would make some sense.

James: That's a good point. Thinking about the fuzziness between disapproval and anger, and affection.

Some people you're close with, there's sometimes the element of disapproval, skepticism, or whatever. You're never quite sure when someone might disapprove or be skeptical of you.

James: That was something that I didn't, uh, that it was okay to be with, my friend. We were close, but it wasn't threatening to say I think you're screwing up here, I think you're doing wrong, you're off base.

Did he say that to you, or you to him?

James: Either way. We would attend each other when that happened, and not feel hurt and rejected.

Do you have anyone else in your life to take his place?

James: Yes.

So this (right hand drawing) represents more than one person. There are other men in your life you can be open with.

James: Uh huh. Yeah. The person I'm thinking of, we didn't really have this sort of relationship (pointing to middle drawing) because it got cut short, you know. The height of our relationship was in adolescence and early twenties, then we were separated. There were a lot of life experiences that we didn't get to share. I hadn't progressed to the point where I was looking into myself, trying to improve myself, and worked through some inner conflicts. I was really hung up back here when I knew him, so he never saw a lot of this side of me (pointing to middle drawing). And I wasn't free to see that side of him.

That's a recent development with you, the freer part.

James: Uh huh. In the past five years or so, where I feel comfortable with touching other males, having them touch me, having regular meaningful discussions where we can approve or disapprove of each other. And where I can go to other men for advice, like as a mentor or something.

It sounds like you like that development, that progression.

James: Yes, it's very valuable. This (red upper left drawing) is the relationship I feel I have with my boss right now. That's how I see him quite a bit, judgmental and false.

You can't trust him.

James: Yeah. If I got this way (middle drawing) too much, it would be used against me.

What do you think he would do to you?

James: I think he's already doing it to a certain extent, covertly. But I think he'd act like everything was okay, like this (pointing to right hand green drawing) but remain this way (left hand red drawing) on the inside, and kind of shut me off. I've seen this very disapproving side come out a few times. But I don't think it's because of me, it's just the way he is. I've got to stay over here (pointing to bottom right photo) with him quite a bit. Actually, the way I present myself is more like this (pointing to left-hand photo and negatives), either shadow or transparent, just not too visible sometimes.

Well, if you feel like changing this art work you certainly could, add to it or change it. If you still feel like something is missing, you may discover what it is and add to it some time.

James: Now that I've got it up here I see how it corresponds to my life.

You might want to put it up where you can see it.

James: Like in my room?

Some place as a reminder.

James: I may do that. It will give me a little map.

James later completed a poster depicting his relationship to women (not shown). James has had a stormy relationship with women and has resorted to physical force, as he explains in the therapy session. The poster is much larger than the one just described, and included pictures cut out of magazines, as well as five photographs of himself and five drawings of women on red or yellow construction paper. Here is a transcript of the therapy session focused on that poster:

Go ahead and describe your art work, and if I think of some questions, I'll ask.

James: Yes. This is "Who am I in relationship to women." When I came here last year, one of the things I wanted to work on was the anger that I was experiencing in my relationships with women. That's one of the first things I put here in the corner. (The upper left corner is a cluster of drawings and photographs mounted on red construction paper. There is a drawing on red construction paper of an angry woman, a photograph of James under that, mounted on a background of red, and to the immediate right, another photograph of James's body, with a large angry red face drawn above the body). The pictures that I posed for myself, I make an angry, disapproving look, with a tense body posture. I tried to capture that feeling with a pose. There is another one up here, with the body posture, but I didn't like the face so I drew a face on there, that I thought was like me, that I might look or feel. I get that way with women, in particular, my wife. We would get in arguments, and I would feel my emotions get out of control. This (angry woman drawing) is her at the same time, showing an angry, disapproving, accusing look.

I cut this picture out (a magazine photograph of a basketball coach looking angry), the coach, because I thought it was similar. If you can see closely, his face is very red, with a lot of tension, and that's how I felt sometimes when I got in an argument. Like close to an angry explosion. But I see this man here (the coach) doing it in a controlled setting. He's expressing himself, like I would like to do sometimes, emotionally, without the fear of the consequences. As you can see, there's other women involved (women basketball players in background).

This picture that I put in the center, at the bottom (large drawing of a woman on yellow construction paper, embracing a photographic image of James lying on a couch), the picture that I posed for, relaxed, withdrawn, the lazy me, and this woman, who has her arms around me, is taking care of me. Remember we talked about one of my relations with females is that I want to be taken care of, mothered. That's probably pretty accurate. I expect women sometimes to do something for me . . . just do something for me, maybe that I can't do for myself or that I need for them to do. It involves some kind of emotional support, or to help me with certain areas of my life that I don't feel too good about. It's the dependent me, in my relationship with women.

This picture down here (drawing in lower left corner of a woman with yellow hair cut from construction paper) is just . . . this one I put together because I liked it. I thought it goes with this area. I put it together with this neat little paper that I found—made hair out of it.

Over on the other side (right side of poster) represents another dimension of female relationships that I have. This little picture here in the middle (nude female body from a magazine, with a drawn head on blue construction paper) is kind of transitional between this angry state over here (left-hand cluster) and this more affectionate, playful state (right side of poster) and sexual area. Over here on the right (photo of James mounted on red construction paper background) I tried to . . . it's more of a relaxed face. My forehead is relaxed, my eyes are open, I'm curious, attentive, sensitive, and reactive. That is, this is how I feel when I am completely with somebody and I have an idea who they are and enjoy being myself and being with them. This is just a playful picture, something that I wish I could do more (magazine picture of a couple dancing). This fellow here is enjoying dancing and it looks like he is making a playful face and strutting around with this lady. I've got a fear of dancing, but it's something I would like to do more, something I have avoided several times but it is a playful activity.

Do you feel awkward when you dance, or do you dance at all?

James: I haven't for a long time. It's probably a matter of just going and doing it. I really enjoy it when I do. I would feel better if I could practice, take a lesson or something. So this looks like a fun picture, a fun activity.

This picture here (picture of the back of a nude woman standing waist deep in water) I thought was a very sensual, beautiful picture of the female form. Her back is to me, but would be facing me in this other picture, standing in front of her (full face photo of James on poster).

This one on the bottom of my picture down here is a picture of affection and touching (magazine picture of a couple in bed. The man's face is against the woman's neck). The two people are obviously very relaxed, touching.

Over here (far right side of poster board, on blue construction paper) I tried to draw a smiling pair of lips. A picture of a female smile.

I think I did a little better on this one (female face on yellow construction paper, with hair cut from gold foil), a female face.

That's a very pleasant, accepting face.

James: Uh huh, uh huh. This is a picture that I took, had taken of me, that is the way I see myself presenting myself for the first time to women (the photo shows James half hidden, leaning out of a doorway. It is mounted in the lower right corner of the poster board). It is curiosity, it is friendliness, you can see I'm opening the door and making a first impression. I'm usually more comfortable with first impressions than with later impressions, so I feel pretty relaxed. I kind of recapture that feeling from time to time as I get to know somebody. I pretend that I am meeting them for the first time and each impression is the first impression. Also this is me opening the door on a relationship, approaching and asking if it is okay for me to come a little bit nearer. Which is an aspect that I like to remember in more intimate relationships, to respect female's personal space, to always approach with that attitude. Can I come a little closer? Can I get to know you? (long pause)

Do you have some clues to the anger part, what triggers that? When you put this poster together, you started out on that, the anger side.

James: Uh huh (long pause).

Well, let me ask that in a different way. Was this anger with one person, your ex-wife, or more than one?

James: It's been more than one. It's been more than once.

Have you ever gone so far as to hit a woman?

James: Uh huh.

More than once?

James: Uh huh.

As I heard you earlier, you want to get to the point where you can express anger, but in a more controlled way, without hitting somebody. That's represented by the picture of the coach there who's yelling and obviously angry but not hitting anybody.

James: Not angry *at* anybody.

Have you had any experiences when you felt angry and were able to control it?

James: Yes I have, and in fact the only . . . now that I think about it the only times I have not controlled my anger was at select times in two marriages and a couple of times with my children. Of course, when I say not control, it's not like I had no control. After a point I had no control, but I didn't have the kind of control I wanted. I had control enough to stop after an initial outburst. If I hit somebody, it wasn't like repeatedly hitting somebody. It was like . . . it wasn't like even hitting somebody except in the case of my children. It was like three times really hard, harder than I should have. With my wife it was like grabbing her by the shoulders or by the hair and just holding her tight while I yelled at her to kind of control her activity. So there was some control there. I still felt very badly about the point which I didn't have control. I wouldn't say I was completely out of control.

Was it related to her not taking care of you, or not being willing to take care of you?

James: I think it was related in some way, because of course it was during an argument and she wasn't responding the way I wanted her to. She was angry and disapproving of me and wouldn't back off at all. She was hollering and screaming. That's just how I chose to react to it.

Is that your second wife or your first wife?

James: Both.

What's your fantasy? If your anger really got out of control, what do you think you might do?

James: That's a private thought, that I reserve for fantasy time.

Okay.

James: I have a fear of hurting somebody. Yeah, I have a fear of hurting somebody. I have come close to it before, and could do it very easily, physically, to the point that I have engaged in physical violence and physical control. I realize that potential because I don't want to do that. It makes me want to have control over how I express anger.

I'll tell you what I don't see here, if you're interested.

James: Un huh.

First of all, I see aggressive relationships and anger. I see a lot of intimacy, sexual intimacy, touching. What I don't see are equal, mutual, respectful relationships like working together for example, or going for a walk. Did that occur to you when you were making this poster, and you decided not to include it, or...

James: It did. I was looking for some pictures of some games or something, some people playing games together. That was one of the last things I was going to put on here. Or doing some sort of tasks together. I didn't know how to construct that. That is something that was lacking in the close relationships I have had and that I have wanted to have more of. Enjoying simple things together.

I was wondering how that might relate to the anger and aggression. If your fundamental orientation is toward either being taken care of, or intimacy, and the woman in your life doesn't want either one of those relationships, but something more Platonic or equal, then I wonder if that might trigger in her some disapproval of you and that, in turn, might make you angry. That's why I asked you awhile ago if you could pinpoint what led up to those aggressive episodes.

James: In my two marriages, so much...it seems like...well, in my first marriage and a few years of my second marriage, I was actively practicing my alcoholism and drug addiction and I didn't make time for too many recreational type activities where I included my wife.

When you did include her in your activity, it was either intimate activities or the more being taken care of kind of thing, you know what I am saying?

James: Well, yes, it was either intimate or on task, that stuff around the house. A lot of it was emotional dependence on my part and a fair amount of arguments. I don't remember too many fun times. In my second marriage, when we had children together, I can remember doing some things together. The last few years, I had hopes that this marriage was gonna work out. It seemed like there was new potential for some new aspects of the relationship. I guess just too much water had gone under the bridge. There were a lot of resentments and a lot of open wounds still. It seems like our communication started digressing into this angry mode more and more where the frequency would increase, and there was too much resentment just to go out and do things together. There was also financial strain and job uncertainty. Arguments over division of labor and finances. There was no outlet except what we would do with the children. Very seldom would we just go out and enjoy each other, go to a movie or go for a walk. When we did, it was okay and a pretty good activity.

What does that tell you about future relationships with women?

James: I think to try to explore areas of common interest first and to try to find out what possibly we could enjoy doing together. There is a lot of stress and strain in life, in my life in particular, and I do have a need to be able to do this kind of thing, it's so enjoyable and relaxing.

I think we're really quick to jump into bed, to jump into the intimacy part of it and not give much thought to the more nonintimate sort of interests you were talking about. We end up looking for somebody to go to bed with or somebody to take care of us.

James: For a long time, that's how I found my worth in a relationship. In my sexual performance, or in the amount I thought they desired me or were available to me sexually. And I felt like I made a lot of progress in the last eight months of this separation. I went through a lot of loneliness and feeling a lot of need to be with somebody sexually, but I haven't gone out and pursued that in a relationship. I have just let that be for a time because I realize that I have a way of using people for becoming dependent in that area to the exclusion of other areas, so I've not gone out in pursuit of that kind of relationship. I've gotten involved in some other things I am interested in. That's a good clue that you just gave me, what that tells me about future relationships.

Just to summarize, what I would suggest to you that might trigger the anger, is that you are relating to women either by, "you take care of me" or "you go to bed with me." If neither one of these needs of dependency or intimacy is being met, then your anger is triggered.

James: I can see a lot in that, because not just either you go to bed with me or take care of me, it may be more general than that. I do think I have trouble thinking of some aspect of my relationship with women that's in between being violently rejected and being intimate with and sexually accepted, and taken care of.

One way you handle that is to fantasize that it is the beginning of the relationship when everything is wide open and possibilities are pretty much endless. When you first meet a woman you are curious and open to all sorts of possibilities, and later on when you get to know her better you sort of fantasize that you are meeting her for the first time. It's almost like you don't want to narrow down too much. I'm suggesting to you that the way you narrow down the relationship is toward those two possibilities, intimacy or dependency, rather than toward more mutual respect. I don't really mean you, I think we all do that. Men treat women in those two ways. Cook for me, clean the house, let's go to bed.

James: Well, I'm curious and interested in finding out more about a relationship with mutual respect and give and take.

I expect they'll discuss it, women will, if you ask.
James: (Laughing) Isn't that a kind of dependency? I say to a woman, tell me what mutual respect is.

As you can see, James took full advantage of the photo art therapy medium to provide a visual referent and focal point for his self-understanding with respect to his relations with men and women. His own photographs and public photographs from magazines, along with other art media, helped him to construct the complex and subtle orientations he has with men and women into a visual form that enabled James to gain some new perspective on his relationships.

From the therapist's point of view, the posters also provided a ready reference for the relationships discussed and depicted by James. Both the therapist and James could readily see the emotions, assumptions, and expectations that James brings to his relationships with men and women.

Chapter 3

PERSONA

The term "persona" is taken from Greek drama wherein an actor would don a mask of a character in order to portray that character. In Jungian theory the persona is that mask that we present to others. In Jung's words, "The persona is a complicated system of relations between individual consciousness and society, fittingly enough a kind of mask, designed on the one hand to make a definite impression upon others, and, on the other, to conceal the true nature of the individual" (Collected Works, Vol. 7, p. 190). Further, he wrote (Collected Works, Vol. 7) that fundamentally the persona is not real. It is an illusion, a compromise between society and the individual as to what the individual should appear to be. The persona presents as an office, a title, an occupation, an identity that *appears* to be real, yet is simply a two-dimensional reality. Consider this: We ask, "What do you *do?*" The answer is, "I *am* an engineer." The occupation has become an identity.

Jung went on to suggest that it is absolutely necessary for one to tear down the persona in order for individuation to occur. As long as one hides behind a title, an office, a name, she is denying herself the opportunity to become a truly unique individual. When one's personality *is* the persona, one is merely a cardboard two-dimensional figure, without depth or substance.

However, the development and maintenance of the persona is a practical necessity. Society demands, in the interests of predictability, that we present a two-dimensional front to the world. Good manners and practicality dictate the presentation of a mask. In order to achieve our goals, we must hide our private life behind a public mask. Social living requires it. This familiar division between public life and private life divides our consciousness, yet another example of the tension of opposites that Jung insists is the source of energy in the human psyche. It is yet another tension that requires transcendence. If a person hides behind the mask to such an extent that she denies her private life, she is an artificial person. Conversely, friends and acquaintances do not want to be bombarded by private revelations all of the time. A compromise is necessary and unavoidable. Too often, the compromise is lopsided, toward allowing the persona to take over.

What are the consequences of allowing the persona to rule the personality? In extreme instances: neurosis. Jung made the point that a person "cannot get rid of himself in favour of an artificial personality without punishment. Even to attempt to do so brings on, in all ordinary cases, unconscious reactions in the form of bad moods, affects, phobias, compulsive ideas, backslidings, vices, etc." (Collected Works, Vol. 7, p. 192). It is not a good idea to ignore the totality of one's personality in favor of the persona. It would follow, then, that recognizing and tearing down the persona would be beneficial. In our view, the important thing is to have a choice, whether to present a persona or not in any given instance, and to have that choice free from psychopathological symptoms of anxiety, compulsions, depression, and so forth. In order to have a choice, one must first have knowledge of oneself.

Part of knowing oneself is knowing one's persona, and the corresponding private life behind the persona. We have developed an extensive program to help a client acquire such knowledge. We call the program the "self-portrait box." The persona can be arbitrarily divided into six parts; the physical persona, the spiritual persona, the family persona, the social persona, the occupational persona, and the emotional persona. Each of the six sides of the box represents one of these facets of the persona.

Keyes (1974) reported on a technique that she developed called "The Self Box" which is similar to the "self-portrait box" but does not necessarily use photographs. Keyes instructed people to place inside the box something symbolic of what is kept hidden and to paint or paste pictures or favorite objects on the outside of the box that are symbols of what is visible to others.

The self-portrait box, because it is divided into six parts of two sides each, takes six–twelve different sessions or one very lengthy one, such as a weekend workshop. Some people prefer to approach the box one side at a time, once per week. Other people do not like to stay in an unfinished state for several weeks and want to finish the box in one or two sessions. The therapist should be flexible with respect to the timing of the activity, as much as is practical.

Persona Assignment

In order to carry out the assignment, the therapist must have a camera and film, one 8″ × 8″ × 8″ cardboard box (we find 8″ or 9″ square boxes to be ideal, but other sizes can be used), twelve 8″ square pieces of poster board or drawing paper, a pencil, and assorted art materials, glue and scissors. Boxes of various sizes can be bought at packaging supply stores. Shoe boxes or other available boxes can be used, as well. One participant used a fruit packing crate.

The client is asked to label, in pencil, the outside of the box with the words Public Physical Self, Public Social Self, Public Family Self, Public Occupational Self, Public Emotional Self, and Public Spiritual Self, one on each side. On the inside of the box the client labels the corresponding sides with Private Physical Self, Private Social Self, and so forth opposite the Public labels for each side. The client then has a cube with the six persona facets on the outside and six facets of her private life on the inside.

As with the other assignments described in this book, clients work in pairs if in a group setting, otherwise with the therapist. The client chooses one of the Public sides to begin. It does not really matter which one, but clients seem to have a preference, probably depending on which is the least demanding. Conversely, some people choose to tackle the most difficult first. We encourage people to begin with the facet they are most comfortable with so that excessive anxiety can be avoided. The client then decides on a body pose that would demonstrate that public persona. Suppose, for the sake of discussion, that the client chooses the Public Physical Self. He might depict himself in a jogging pose, showing to the public that he is interested in a healthy life style. It does not hurt to exaggerate the pose. The client strikes the pose and the therapist or partner takes the snapshot.

The artwork is not done directly on the box, for practical reasons. People sometimes want to make changes, and change on the box itself is difficult. Also, it is hard to work in the cramped quarters of the inside of the box. The client mounts the photograph on one of the poster board or drawing paper squares, after cutting out the image, if desired. The photo can be augmented with whatever background is needed, from the other art supplies such as marking pens and construction paper. In the example we are discussing, the client might draw in a jogging track or street scene, or perhaps a gym. After the work is completed, it is glued on the appropriate side of the box.

Following the Public Self assignment, the client tackles the Private Self assignment. Often, that assignment is at a later session because it may take an hour or more to complete each side of the box. Following the Physical Self example, suppose the client privately is aware that he has serious hypertension and a history of heart disease in his family. His father and two uncles have died of heart attacks before age 50. Privately he is concerned about his potential for heart disease. He does not generally share this private knowledge with other people, feeling that his medical history is his own business. The client might reflect this concern by a body pose that shows him grasping his chest as if having a heart attack. The partner or therapist captures the pose with a snapshot, and the client then mounts and augments the photo as before. The completed artwork is glued on the inside of the box opposite the Public Physical Self side.

The therapist and client have an ongoing discussion during the photography and artwork, with the client's choices of poses, art materials, and art production as the stimuli for the discussion. As with any art therapy, the emphasis is on the psychological process rather than the aesthetics.

Having completed one side of the box, inside and out, the client chooses another side and repeats the process, outside first, then inside. Eventually, after several sessions, the client has a self-portrait cube with public persona on the outside and private life on the inside. If the client wants the inside to remain private, he can glue the box lid shut, so that no one knows that there are additional photographs inside.

During the process, a curious thing happens. The client begins by making a fairly clear and obvious distinction between public and private. As the photography and artwork progress, it becomes less and less clear which is public and which is private, and it becomes less important to keep the public and private selves separate. In other words, the persona begins to break down. Several people have even put handles on the box lid, an invitation for other people to examine the private contents.

From a theoretical perspective, it is not perfectly clear why the persona begins to break down as a result of the self-portrait box assignment. One possibility has to do with secrets and was addressed by Jung in 1929 (Collected Works, Vol. 16). In that article he wrote:

Anything concealed is a secret. The possession of secrets acts like a psychic poison that alienates their possessor from the community.

A secret shared with several persons is as beneficial as a merely private secret is destructive. The latter works like a burden of guilt, cutting off the unfortunate possessor from communion with his fellows. But, if we are conscious of what we are concealing, the harm done is decidedly less than if we do not know what we are repressing—or even that we have repressions at all.

To cherish secrets and hold back emotion is a psychic misdemeanor for which nature finally visits us with sickness—that is, when we do these things in private. But when they are done in communion with others they satisfy nature and may even count as useful virtues. It is only restraint practised for oneself alone that is unwholesome. It is as if man had an inalienable right to behold all that is dark, imperfect, stupid, and guilty in his fellow men—for such, of course, are the things we keep secret to protect ourselves. It seems to be a sin in the eyes of nature to hide our inferiority—just as much as to live entirely on our inferior side. There would appear to be a sort of conscience in mankind which severely punishes every one who does not somehow and at some time, at whatever cost to his virtuous pride, cease to defend and assert himself, and instead confess himself fallible and human. Until he can do this, an impenetrable wall shuts him off from the vital feeling that he is a man among other men (pp. 57–59).

So, admitting the private inside of the box to the therapist and possibly other therapy group members is wholesome and therapeutic, for keeping a truly private secret is psychically damaging whereas a secret shared with a few others leads to a sense of communion and the lessening of the need to defend and protect oneself.

Jung's discussion of secrets, incidentally, seems to us to be germane to the practice of group psychotherapy. Sharing secrets with other group members, at least up to a point, would be therapeutic, according to him. It seems contradictory that Jung was steadfastly against group analysis. See Chapters 11, 12, and 13 for more discussion of group photo art therapy.

Harry

In Chapter 6, the reader will hear about one of Harry's dreams, and in Chapter 8, Harry shares his artwork concerning conflicts. There is also a reproduction of one of Harry's posters in Chapter 9, having to do with apathy and cyclical depression. During the same therapy program, but several weeks earlier, Harry completed a self-portrait box, working with a partner. The entire box took about 20 hours to complete, over a period of six weeks. Some of the work was done with his partner and some on his

own as ideas came to him. One view of the box is presented in Figure 3-1.
Harry's comments about his self-portrait box follow:

> The self-portrait box was difficult for me, but very exciting and meaningful.
> I feel attached to it and have it displayed in my home as one would display a
> photo album. My partner was helpful and by talking things over with her
> during the assignment, I was able to understand better and to proceed with the
> project.
>
> I began with the Public Social Self side of the box. As it turned out, this side
> was the easiest for me. Some of the others were more emotional, particularly
> the sides having to do with family. In my social life, I think people see me as
> affable and easy going. I enjoy being with people and prefer to listen rather
> than talk about myself. My photograph shows me standing quietly in a group
> of people, listening and drinking a beer. There are people laughing and
> telling jokes, and there are many different kinds of people. I used magazines
> and cut out pictures of people.
>
> The Private Social Self was fairly easy too. I feel privately that I need to
> spend more time cultivating friendships, so I simply posed for a photograph
> showing me on the telephone, talking with friends.
>
> I can't remember in exactly what order I completed the other sides, except
> that I did the Emotional side last, and never did complete the Public Emo-
> tional Self. I just couldn't seem to come up with a way to do it. I think,
> truthfully, that I hide my emotions a great deal and really do not have much of
> a public emotional side. The art work for my private emotional side came to
> me clearly and easily. I feel that my emotions are a balancing act, so I made a
> teeter-totter and balanced a photo cutout of myself on each end. I made each
> end a different color, one blue and one orange, and colored the background
> these two different colors. I also made the emotional side the bottom of the
> box, believing that emotions are basic. I put the spiritual sides on top.
>
> The spiritual side of myself is a mystery to me. I do not attend church and
> do not belong to or believe in any organized religion. However, working
> through this assignment led me to a couple of fairly clear conclusions. Publicly,
> I profess to believe that God is love, and that the love flows freely between God
> and man and among people. I tried to show that by posing with a wicker heart,
> that freely allowed anything in it to flow in and out. The flowing of love in and
> out is symbolized by valentine hearts. I also ringed the edges of the box on that
> side with small cut out valentine hearts. On the other hand, I do not really
> believe that people love one another. The papers are full of murder and
> assault. History is replete with man's cruelty to man. I guess I *want* to believe
> that God is love, and perhaps in the long run that belief will prove true.
>
> Privately, I see God and my own spirituality in nature. My partner had
> given me a photograph she had taken of sunrise on Galveston beach, and I
> used that to show the spirituality of nature. That photograph is on the inside
> of the lid of the box, and is the first thing that can be seen when the box is
> opened. That photograph is especially important for me because it was a gift

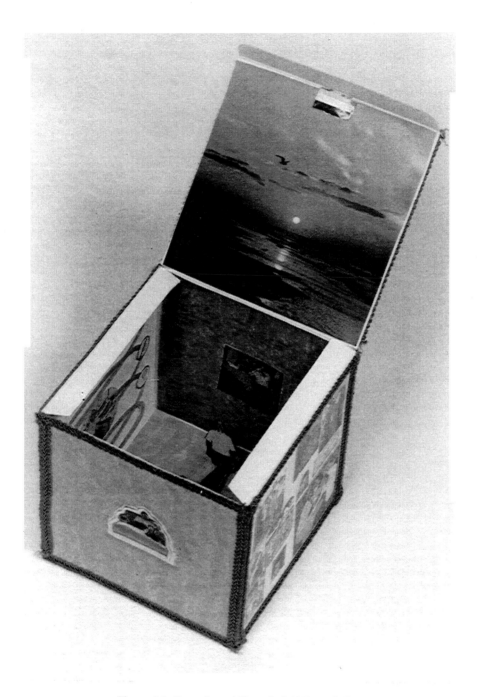

Figure 3-1. One view of Harry's Self-Portrait Box.

from a close friend, and I often walk on the beach in the early morning to watch the sun come up, and I try to find a quiet time to watch the sunset whenever I can.

Publicly, people see me as physically very relaxed. My friends and colleagues often remark on how relaxed I seem. And I am relaxed. For my Public Physical side, I posed for a photograph lounging in a chair, reading a book. That is probably an accurate portrayal.

Privately, I worry about growing older. I am forty six now and feel fit, but my brain is not as efficient as it once was. I forget things and have to rely more on notes. I sometimes completely forget important information. Actually, that is not so much a function of aging as it is something else. I have always been forgetful and have been embarrassed from time to time by forgetting invitations or other events. I can't tell if my memory is getting worse, but I think it is. Apparently it happens to everybody, but that doesn't make it any less of a problem for me.

This memory problem is more or less private, because it can't be seen except indirectly. I worry that people may misinterpret. If I forget somebody's name, that person may think I am being a snob. I tried to show, on the inside of the box, the private nature of this particular physical concern by drawing in the outlines of a brain with the universal sign for "no" superimposed on it.

The Occupational or Professional side of my box concerns the brain too. I think of my profession as involving three main activities; teaching, consulting, and writing. All of these activities require me to think and remember. For the public side, I drew a brain in the center, and a triangle surrounding it, connecting the three activities. I posed for three photographs; one teaching at a blackboard, one composing at a word processor, and one consulting with another person.

Privately, I think I try to do too many different things in my profession. My profession is the world of ideas, and sometimes there are simply too many of them. I can pretty much organize my time any way I see fit, and it is possible for me to spread myself too thin by engaging in too many ideas and activities at once. I tried to show this by drawing a helix around myself seated at my desk. The helix contains light bulbs representing ideas. Some light bulbs are green, symbolizing unripe ideas that have to be investigated. Some bulbs are black, representing ideas that turned out to be duds. Still others are bright, symbolizing bright ideas that turned out to be good ones. There are others that were bright initially, but for some reason didn't stay that way, and faded.

All of these ideas can lead to research projects or other endeavors. It can get to be confusing. Because I am reluctant to narrow myself to any one pursuit, sometimes it seems overwhelming. I addressed this personality trait in my work on conflicts (see Chapter 8). I am always struggling with this tendency to try to do too many different things at once.

For the Public Family side of the box, I relied on snapshots from family albums. I included my original family and my current family. At the upper left, I glued a photograph of my mother and father and brother and sister, taken about 1948. Just below that I put on pictures of my grandfather and his dog, and two of my grandmothers. I lived with my grandparents quite a lot when I was growing up, and think of them as my parents. I have a picture of my mother peering out from behind a shrub. My mother was always in the background like that, and was a self-effacing person. She died of cancer when I was sixteen years old.

My original family takes up most of the left side of the panel. In the middle I pasted a photograph of myself and my son when he was just learning to walk. Somehow, he bridges the gap between my original family and my current family. I also have a picture of my wife, and a second picture of my wife and our son. My mother-in-law is an important part of our family now, so I included a picture of her with our son. They spend a lot of time together. I also pasted on a picture of our foster son, who is now living in another city, and a picture of the tombstone on my grandmother's grave. That gravestone seems to represent all of my family members who have died. My mother and father, several uncles and aunts, and all of my grandparents are now deceased. I still have a step-grandmother living.

I have a lot of private family feelings regarding my original family. There was a great deal of turmoil in my family. My father was in mental hospitals much of the time, and he was a terror when he was home. We children were all glad when he was gone for awhile and we tiptoed around him carefully when he was home. Our mother kept the home together and when she died, it was a disaster. I showed the private family side of the box by pasting a large picture of my mother's gravestone in the middle of the panel, with a photo of myself, crying, superimposed on top of it. Even though she died thirty years ago, I have never really gotten over it. My brother and sister haven't either. We relied on her to take care of us and to act as a buffer between our father and us. After she died, the family split up and we all went different directions.

The persona self-portrait box, for Harry, was a very meaningful and complicated process. He worked on it for about 20 hours, by himself and with his partner. Not only did he use instant photographs taken by his partner, but also photographs out of his family albums and photographs from magazines. It was a moving experience for him, especially the parts having to do with his family.

Other people who have completed the self-portrait box also report that it is a very important experience. Helga (see Chapters 1 and 4) completed a self-portrait box and now has it hanging on display in her home, much as one would display a photo album. She also incorporated photographs from her family albums.

Chapter 4

THE SHADOW

The shadow, in Jungian psychology, is the base, dark side to our personality. It is the denied part, the part that can be glimpsed from time to time, but cannot be directly confronted without effort. The shadow is that part of our personality that remains unconscious, that we avoid, that we are not pleased with, that we try to hide from ourselves and others. There is evil lurking in the shadow, and also energy, creativity, and knowledge.

Another side of the shadow is called positive shadow. This aspect of shadow projects one's unexplored or undeveloped positive qualities onto another. This positive shadow, which like negative shadow is often accompanied by strong emotions, might signify one's unfulfilled life, and can be identified by powerful feelings such as admiration or envy.

Marie-Louise von Franz (1974, p. 5) describes shadow as "simply a 'mythological' name for all that within me of which I cannot directly know." Hall reminded us that the word shadow does not mean something evil, but simply refers to what is thrown into the "shade" by that which stands in the "light" of our consciousness. In a more humorous vein, Hall (1990) defined shadow as "that which I'm sure I don't have, but suspect I do, and if I do, I hope nobody notices."

Jung discussed the shadow in several writings and lectures as the entry to the unconscious. "The darkness which clings to every personality is the door into the unconscious and the gateway of dreams, from which those two twilight figures, the shadow and the anima, step into our nightly visions or, remaining invisible, take possession of our ego-consciousness. A man who is possessed by his shadow is always standing in his own light and falling into his own traps" (Collected Works, Vol. 9, Pt. 1, p. 123). He saw the shadow not only as the entry to the unconscious, but as the very foundation of the personality. "Even our purest and holiest beliefs rest on very deep and dark foundations; after all, we can explain a house not only from the attic downwards, but from the basement upwards, and the latter explanation has the prime advantage of being genetically the more correct, since houses are in fact built bottom-side first, and the beginning of all things is simple and crude" (Collected Works, Vol. 16, p. 64).

Jung clearly felt that it is necessary to confront the shadow in one's personality, and acknowledged how difficult such a confrontation might be. " . . . the meeting with ourselves belongs to the more unpleasant things that can be avoided so long as we can project everything negative into the environment. But if we are able to see our own shadow and can bear knowing about it, then a small part of the problem has already been solved: we have at least brought up the personal unconscious. The shadow is a living part of the personality and therefore wants to live with it in some form. It cannot be argued out of existence or rationalized into harmlessness" (Collected Works, Vol. 16, Pt. 1, p. 20).

Frey-Rohn (1967) also stressed the importance of recognizing one's shadow. She wrote that the personal shadow is a highly important reality, a "dark" factor, which is always present and effective, just as is our shadow from the sun, and which is a part of everything we do. She continued with the assertion that the more we take the shadow into account the more human we will be.

The shadow is difficult to make out and understand. Several years ago, a man in therapy told this story:

> I have been learning about dreams, especially about the technique of confronting the monsters in your nightmares. Last night I had this dream that I was being chased by some shadowy monster, and I thought, in my dream, that I would simply turn around and ask the monster what he wanted of me. In my dream, I turned around quickly, and just as quickly the monster whirled around with me so that it was still behind me, unseen. I tried the turning technique several times, and each time the monster was just as quick as I. I was never able to see what was pursuing me. It remained in the shadow. I guess I was not ready to see that part of my personality. Perhaps later.

Another man, who had been divorced and was not in a present romantic relationship, told of a similar experience, but with a different outcome:

> I dreamed that I was being chased by a mad bull. In my dream I turned around and asked the bull, "What do you want?" The bull, in an apologetic tone, and without seeming frightening at all, answered, "I want you to introduce me to some women." Immediately I was no longer afraid.

In this second instance, the man was ready and able to see the shadow side for what it was, normal sexual desire.

The shadow shows up in dreams, and in other ways also. We tend to project our shadow onto other people, especially those of the same gender as ourselves. If we meet someone and take an immediate and intense dislike to that person, perhaps we are seeing our own shadow. The qualities that we loathe in that other person are expressly those shadow qualities that we will not or cannot admit in ourselves.

It might be that we recognize our shadow after the fact. We may do something that, afterward, makes us feel ashamed or guilty. At the time of the action, however, there was some kind of compelling quality to the situation that seemed to give us no alternative. We often disown these actions after the fact by claiming that we would not have done it if we had been sober, that "something came over me," that "the devil made me do it."

The shadow can take many forms and is present in all of us. As we grow up, we make early judgments about what is "good" and what is "bad." Hall (1986) believes that people make primitive judgments about good and evil as young as six or eight months. Any recognition of "bad" or "evil" in one's own behavior or thoughts tends to be relegated to the shadow as unacceptable. Later on, we may catch glimpses of these unacceptable shadow qualities in our own behavior, attitudes, or thoughts and become anxious about that.

There are several shadow qualities that are immediately recognizable by most of us. The aggressor or warrior is perhaps the most obvious. The aggressor relates to other people with violence or anger, almost exclusively. Teasing, taunting, name calling, scathing comments, as well as outright assault are all aggressive and reflect the aggressor shadow. One thinks of the all-too-common patterns of child abuse and spouse abuse. A subtle variant is passive aggression, where a person stands by and does not prevent injury or violence when it could be prevented, or a person provokes anger in others by acting passively. Teenagers are very good at passive aggression. "Where have you been?" "Out." "What have you been doing?" "Nothing."

Miserliness may lurk in the shadows. Hoarding money is one possibility, but one can be tight with any resource—time, possessions, kindness, even love. Dickens's classic *A Christmas Carol* dealt with this shadow quality in the character of Ebeneezer Scrooge.

Hypocrisy, unnecessary heroics, gluttony, gossiping (possibly a form of aggression), pedantry, seductiveness, thievery, greed, and foolishness are still other shadowy personality traits.

The shadow pervades literature, myth, folk tales, music, art and all of culture. Fairy tales are particularly rich in shadows. Who is not familiar with the evil stepmother, the greedy brothers, the hypocritical, deceiving sisters, the witch? The reader may want to study von Franz (1974) for an analysis of shadow in fairy tales.

It is outside the scope of this book, but we should mention that many writers have addressed the "collective shadow" also. The common experience of mob violence is one example. The chilling news recently of a young black man being beaten to death by a group of white men, simply because they did not like the fact that he had been talking with a white woman, is surely an example of shadow. No doubt that tragedy would never have happened without the collective nature of the group shadow of violence and hatred. In Houston in July, 1991, Paul Broussard was beaten to death by a roving band of men carrying knives and boards studded with nails. He was gay. Another tragic example of the collective shadow.

Institutionalized aggression, war, can be analyzed as collective shadow, also. Witness the unprovoked attack on Kuwait by Saddam Hussein and his army. Certainly Saddam could not have succeeded in the invasion by himself. He needed an army to cooperate with his invasion. The "killing fields" of Cambodia and the holocaust in Europe are other well-known examples of institutionalized aggression.

Although we assume that these shadowy, unacceptable impulses are detrimental to ourselves and others, that is not necessarily the case. The shadow has both positive and negative qualities. There is great energy and creativity bound up in the shadow. Consider aggression. The shadow of aggression is everywhere. It is institutionalized as war. It is abhorred as murder, rape, and assault. Yet we must be able to defend ourselves, with force if necessary. We must assert our rights if we are to live fulfilling lives. Assertiveness, because of "shadow anxiety," is frequently mistaken for unacceptable aggression, as Hall has pointed out (1986). Anger has its place, and tells other people exactly how we feel. Assertiveness is standing up for one's rights without infringing on the rights of others. The recognition and acceptance of the aggressor shadow allows us to be appropriately angry and assertive, and to defend ourselves. Such a recognition and acceptance will not automatically unleash an uncontrolled aggressor on the world. On the contrary, conscious recognition and acceptance of our shadow makes it *less* likely that we will be possessed by it. It is only through retrieving and scrutinizing these customarily negative aspects, recognized in our dreams and projections, that we can accept and integrate our shadow qualities. With this awareness we can begin to make choices, no longer living out the shadow unconsciously.

The purpose of the photo art therapy assignment to be discussed in this chapter is to help the client become more aware of the shadow, and to incorporate that awareness, that transformation from unconscious to conscious, into the ego. Crucial to the therapy, we believe, is the awareness on the part of the client that the shadow is not all evil and malevolent. We stress the fact that shadow is simply parts of one's personality that have been denied and have not come to light, and can be a source of great energy and creativity.

Shadow Exercise

In order to carry out the photo art therapy "shadow" assignment, the therapist meets with the client for one or more sessions and carries out a discussion about the concept of the shadow much like that reported above. Reading about shadow figures in fairy tales with the client is enlightening, because almost everyone is versed in fairy tales from childhood. In workshops we also show slides made from illustrations and other art that depict the shadow. The client is then provided with a sheet of poster board and assorted art supplies, glue and scissors. The therapist has a Polaroid® camera with film for at least two photographs. If the work is in a group, the people are paired off and each pair is given supplies and a camera.

During the discussion about the shadow, the clients probably have an inkling of some shadow parts of their personalities. If not, the therapist asks them to think about times when they have been compelled to do something, or were obsessed with some action or thought. Another hint of the shadow lies in one's choices of movies, music, plays, and books. What particularly excites you, in a secret kind of way? What figure in a fairy tale stirs your emotions? Have you had a dream that featured an ominous character? Remember qualities in other people that you dislike. Perhaps you have those qualities to some extent yourself and don't like to admit it.

When the client has selected one shadow to explore, he is instructed to imagine both ends of a positive-negative dimension related to that shadow quality. When the client has the dimension in mind, then the therapist and client together explore how the client can depict the two ends of the dimension with poses that can be photographed. The client strikes the poses and the therapist or partner takes the picture.

The client can mount the two photographs on the poster board in such a way to depict the positive-negative dimension of the shadow. Any art materials can be used to augment the poster. Some clients use two poster boards and put the negative on one and the positive on the other.

Processing

Processing of the art work goes on between therapist and client while the client is doing the art work, if in individual therapy; or if in a group, between the partners. In our therapy, we do little interpretation of the art, preferring to leave the interpretation to the artist. Be aware that discussing shadow that has just been enlightened can be frightening and embarrassing, and that the client needs time to assimilate the knowledge that is emerging, just as a butterfly needs time to dry her wings after emerging from the cocoon. We encourage the client to simply elaborate on the poster board. We ask about choice of colors and shapes, the choice of poses, and the relationship of the positive to the negative ends of the shadow dimension. We help the client think how to accept negative shadow qualities and possibly to convert those negative qualities to positive ones, and draw parallels to everyday life. Because of the pervasive nature of the shadow, it is possible and even desirable to repeat the assignment with as many different shadow figures as the client is able to recognize. One male client has courageously completed three shadow posters, "The dirty old man," "The pedant," and "The miser."

To illustrate a photo art therapy shadow assignment, we reproduce two posters done by a client, and her verbatim comments about the work. The reproductions are with her permission.

Helga

Helga is a German immigrant who moved to the United States by herself when she was a young woman. She is married and the mother of three grown children. During our discussion of the shadow, Helga identified a personality quality that might be described as excessive formality or rigidity. She carried out the assignment by preparing two posters of herself, one labeled the "Shatten" (Shadow) and the other "Der Befreite Shatten" (The Emancipated Shadow).

About the "shatten" posters (Figures 4-1 and 4-2), Helga says:

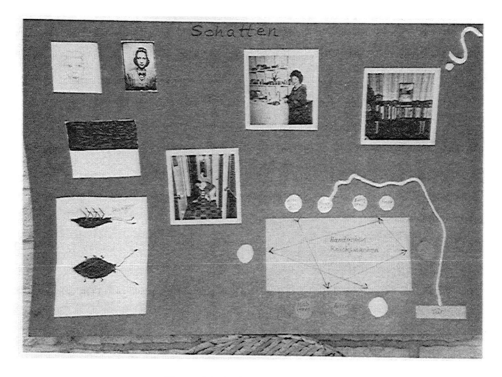

Figure 4-1. Helga's Shadow Poster

Something which was in my life from early on was rigidity. Until far into my adult years things or situations were only black or white, right or wrong. I could often not conceive of a middle path or its variations.

Already as a very young child I had to learn all the etiquette of society. At school I had to tell my teachers at vacation time, "Have a nice summer" or "Merry Christmas," a greeting which none of the other students made. I felt embarrassed having to do this.

When I brought flowers to someone it was important to remove the paper before handing the bouquet to the other person. And, when invited to a coffee or party, I needed to know whom to greet first and whom to shake hands with last. It was appropriate to begin greeting the oldest couple, then the people of middle age and the youngest people last (see the diagram, lower right corner of Figure 4-1).

Within myself I disliked those formalities, because they did not come from the heart. Even though my mother was very loving and always good to us, it was important to my parents that we could conduct ourselves properly within their circle of friends, and thus we were trained like little puppies. We had to curtsy and bow with the greetings. But, already as a child I wondered if the

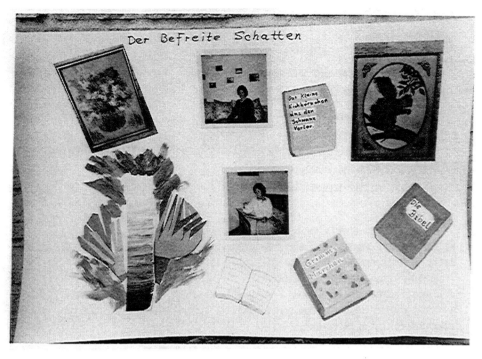

Figure 4-2. Helga's Emancipated Shadow Poster

younger people did not feel hurt when I passed them up in order to greet the older ones first. Of course, all these courtesies were part of the caste system.

This rigidity was then reinforced in school when we had to stand perfectly straight while greeting the teacher when she entered the class. Holding onto the desk was being ridiculed.

A poem by Sophie Reinheimer verifies line by line how children were raised at that time:

The Birthday Congratulant

I should say "good morning" and compliments from mother.
She is inquiring how the godparent is doing.
And the bouquet in from our yard, in case thou would like to know.
But I should wait at the door, should thou have something to say to me.
And, I should greet each one very nicely, but be silent when someone
   speaks,
yet, I should speak clearly, but not scream when I talk.
But, I should not feel ashamed, for I am virtuous and religious.
Though when entering the room, I should take off my cap.
In case someone should give me something, I should say "thank you"
But, I should not constantly look at the birthday cake.

And, nice and slowly I should eat, it would be improper to stuff food in my
   mouth.
And, I almost forgot: I am also to CONGRATULATE.

(Helga spontaneously remembered this poem from her childhood
while preparing the "shatten" poster.)

My rigidity was such, that while combing my hair, each hair had to be in
place. Once, I combed until I fainted. While having my picture taken, I was
asked to look to the right and then left. I only moved my eyes while holding
my head straight.

(The picture in the upper left of Figure 4-1 is a photograph of Helga at
age 16).

I did not feel comfortable among the sometimes stuck up people of the
upper societal class, and I was more drawn to the simple little girls who had
heart. The profession of these children's father was of no concern to me, as
long as the girls treated me nicely.

When I came to America, I stripped myself of this "armor," for I soon
learned about the uncomplicated ways of Americans who do not pay much
attention to this type of etiquette.

At the early years of my marriage I did a lot of cleaning in our new home,
even though we did not have any children for the first five years. A visitor once
remarked to me that any cockroaches would starve because everything was so
clean and shiny. Even in my last month of pregnancy I got on my knees and
shined my parquet floors.

Because we live in a subtropical climate, there are not only beautiful exotic
plants and animals here, but also a lot of bugs which I do not tolerate in my
house.

But, to me, the worst effect of this rigidity was my way of thinking. I always
wanted to read and learn, but did not get time for it because of all the house
and yard work.

Now, our children are grown. And some time ago a big change took place
within me. This change was especially advantageous to our youngest son
who, at the age of 16 was very self-reliant and adventurous, yet conscien-
tious.

To this day, I do not like disarray in our home, but I can tolerate dust, if the
house is otherwise neat and my kitchen is clean. Of course this had its
advantages, for when entering a dirty kitchen in the morning, one could easily
feel nauseated. For my own development this change has been very positive. I
can paint in my studio while things are not put away and I can allow myself to
read even though the leaves in the yard have not been raked.

People like the fine details in my art work. I can paint with broad strokes
with a brush and also work with a pallet knife (the bouquet and the squirrel in
Figure 4-2 are photographs of original art by Helga).

When my children were grown, I began completing my university studies, which I had started before they were born. With so much more flexibility in my thinking, I feel like a child with a new toy. At times I write a little story like "The Little Squirrel Who Lost Its Tail."

Today I view the Bible as well as Grimm's Fairy Tales from a very different perspective, for in both works a lot of symbolism is to be found.

Orderliness, if not carried to extremes, is of value. It is easier to find things in house or office and it is easier to organize everyday life that way.

Helga did these two posters three years ago. In preparation for this book, we interviewed her again, and found that she has completed her bachelor's degree and is now herself teaching. She continues to read and study, and has found time to read many of the books she had put aside. Helga is painting and enjoys her art. Religious or spiritual studies have been important to Helga, and one book, *God's Psychiatry,* has been especially meaningful.

A few months ago she had an insight that seems to be another milestone on her way to emancipating her shadow. While driving home from a university class, it suddenly occurred to Helga that learning did not have to be work, it could be fun! She has come to appreciate her own capabilities. In her words, "I thought everything which was hard and difficult to attain for me was of value. My own innate capabilities and talents seemed worthless because it was easy work for me."

She has made good use of this insight, and has learned to use a computer, and now finds it enjoyable rather that a chore. She has relearned the rules of German grammar and has even found that to be a relatively easy and pleasant task.

As a final comment, we might mention that Helga's choice of shadow is a good example of personality traits or attitudes that, by many people's standards, are not at all bad, evil, or destructive. In fact, some may see her formality and desire for order as a positive thing. For her, however, it was a part of her personality that was compulsive, and interfered with her attempts at a more satisfying life. Helga still has an interest in order and neatness, but the compelling quality is gone.

Chapter 5

ARCHETYPES

THE MAGIC SWAN GEESE

Once upon a time there lived an old man and his wife who had two children, a son and a daughter. On their way to market one day the mother said, "Daughter, we will bring you back a new dress, a kerchief, and a sugar bun. But be very careful. Watch over your baby brother, and do not leave the house. Baba Yaga's magic swan geese have been seen flying near our village."

The girl entertained her little brother for a time after her parents left, but then her friends called to her to play, and she took him out onto the grass where she could watch him. As she become involved in the games, the girl forgot all about her baby brother sitting in the grass and her parents' warning. The magic swan geese swooped down, seized the child, and flew away with him.

When the girl went back for her brother, he was nowhere to be seen. She looked around the yard, and he was not there. She looked into the house; he was not there. The girl became very frightened. She called out his name and then began to sob. What would her father and her mother say? They had trusted her to care for her baby brother. The girl looked toward the skies. In the distance she could see Baba Yaga's swan geese flying over the dark forest. "Oh, they've taken my brother," she cried, "my sweet baby brother." And she rushed toward the forest where she had seen the geese. She remembered the awful stories that she had heard about the terrible witch Baba Yaga who is eight feet tall and devours little children, and she ran faster.

As she ran, the girl saw a stove. "Stove, stove, tell me, whither have the geese flown?" The stove answered, "I will tell you if you eat my cake of rye." "Oh, no," the girl said, "at my house we don't even eat cakes of wheat." So the stove did not tell her. She continued to run, and soon came to an apple tree. "Apple tree, apple tree, whither have the geese flown," asked the girl. "I will tell you if you eat one of my wild apples," said the tree. "Oh, no," said the girl, "at my house we don't even eat sweet apples." Next she saw a river of milk with shores of pudding. "River of milk, shores of pudding, whither have the geese flown?" she asked. "I will tell you if you will eat my simple pudding and some milk." "Oh, no," she said, "at my father's house we don't even eat cream."

After a time, the girl became confused and afraid. The woods were dark, and she had lost her way. Then she met a hedgehog. Gingerly, she tiptoed close to him and whispered, "Hedgehog, hedgehog, have you not seen whither the geese have flown?" "Thither," said the hedgehog, and he showed her. She ran in the direction he pointed and saw Baba Yaga's hut sitting on three chicken legs that moved about. Her little brother was playing nearby, while the witch, Baba Yaga, snored loudly. The geese were roosting on the roof of the hut.

The girl quickly snatched up her brother, and began to run. But the magic swan geese awakened from their sleep and began to honk and flap their wings. Baba Yaga awakened from the noise and screamed, "Come back! Come back! I'll have the both of you for my dinner!"

With Baba Yaga and the geese in pursuit, the girl ran to the river of milk with shores of pudding. "Little mother river, hide me!" she cried. "If you eat my pudding," was the river's reply. So she ate the pudding, and the river hid her beneath its shore, and the witch and her geese didn't find them. When she felt she was safe, the girl ran on, carrying her brother. It wasn't long before Baba Yaga, flying in her mortar, spurring it with the pestle, and sweeping along with her broom caught sight of them again. The girl saw the apple tree and begged, "Apple tree, apple tree, little mother, hide me!" "If you eat my wild apple," the tree said. So the girl ate the apple, and the tree covered her with its branches and leaves. And again she was hidden from her pursuers.

When she felt she was safe, the girl began to run carrying her brother. He was getting heavy. Soon the girl could hear the whirring and honking of geese. They were very close. Fortunately, the stove was in her path. "Madam Stove, please hide me!" she begged. "If you will eat my cake of rye," the stove said. The girl quickly ate the cake, then crawled into the stove with her brother and sat there. She could hear the wings of the geese whirring overhead and loud and angry cursing from the witch, but she and her brother stayed safely hidden within the belly of the stove.

After the noises stopped, the stove announced that the path was clear for the girl. She ran home with her brother in her arms, arriving just before her parents returned with her new dress and the wonderful sugar buns.

We admit that we have taken some poetic license in reporting the story of *The Magic Swan Geese*. In the original Russian version, Baba Yaga's swan geese pursue the child and her brother (Afanesev, 1973). In our altered version, we include Baba Yaga in the chase. Baba Yaga appears in European fairy tales in many guises. She is called the Bony-legged One and sometimes the Golden-legged. She is usually associated with birds in the stories, either as her helpers or her foes. She flies through the air on her broom, driving a mortar and spurring it along with her pestle. Baba Yaga not only eats little children, but is also known to devour grown people, too. As evidence of her unusual eating habits, there are usually human bones lying around in her yard.

Baba Yaga's house stands on chicken feet and moves around. Often, a visitor coming to Baba Yaga's house says the words, "Little hut, little hut, stand with your back to the woods, and your front to me!" Then the hut turns around. Around the house are twelve stakes and on eleven of these stakes are human heads; only one stake remains bare (and that stake, my dear readers, is for your imagination).

On the other hand, in some Baba Yaga tales, she is a wise woman who gives advice to princes on their quests; princes who address her as "grandmother." There also are times when several "Baba Yagas" appear in a story, each having different personalities. Undoubtedly, the Baba Yaga tales have also had another purpose throughout the ages, that of instilling fear into little children who do not mind their parents.

Baba Yaga and the other characters in "The Magic Swan Geese" fairy tale are examples of archetypes, portraying exaggerated patterns of behavior. These patterns of behavior, found in myths, fantasies, dreams, and fairy tales, are typically one-dimensional figures and portray classical ways that we act and interact with others. Jung describes archetypes as a grouping of archaic characters containing *mythological motifs,* in form as well as meaning. These motifs, according to Jung, appear in pure form in fairy tales, myths, and legends. Jung (Collected Works, Vol. 18) says that some of the better-known motifs include figures of the Hero, the Redeemer, the Dragon (which is always connected with the Hero), and the Whale or the Monster (who swallows the Hero). Uncompromising evil comes in such forms as witches, step-mothers, gnomes, and giants; while good is often represented by the princess, the hero, the innocent child or the naive bumpkin.

These archetypal images seem to have the ability to hold the attention of persons of all ages: children, adolescents, and adults alike. For example, hospitalized acting-out adolescents, who one might normally think would reject such "childish" literature as fairy tales, conversely become intrigued with the stories and listen to them intently, according to experiences of the authors and other therapists who have used fairy tales in their work. Jung says that since the archetypes are instinctive, inborn forms of psychic behavior, they influence the psychic processes in a powerful manner. And unless and until the conscious, rational mind intervenes in the processes, a repeat of behavioral patterns will continue as they have in the past, no matter if they are to the advantage or disadvantage of the individual (Collected Works, Vol. 18).

We like Roberts's definition of the archetypes in his *Tales for Jung folks* (1983, p. 8): "Any discussion of Jungian psychology is incomplete without mention of the archetypes, which are formless *unconscious quantities* which acquire *conscious qualities* of various forms. According to Jung, the term 'archetype' is often misunderstood as meaning certain definite mythological images or motifs. But these are nothing more than conscious representations; it would be absurd to assume that such variable representations could be inherited. The archetype is a tendency to form such representations of a motif—representations that can vary a great deal in detail without losing their basic pattern."

In a hospital setting, adolescents can draw, paint, sculpt, or create collages while listening to ancient tales of princes and princesses, kings and peasants, embarking on mythical journeys to gain special knowledge or to find secret treasures. As they discuss their art work, these adolescents might associate the tales to events in their own lives, their personal journeys, their own glass mountains that they need to climb. They are also able to relate to the fairy tale motif: that of continuing to strive for what they feel to be important in their lives, to be scrupulously honest (although trickery is acceptable), and to be sensitive to the needs of the creatures of the forest (possibly, their own intuitive natures).

One of the authors (Corbit) used to regularly bring collections of fairy tales to the locked psychiatric unit on which she worked. The adolescents on the unit, as well as staff members, looked forward eagerly to these stories. Patients and staff members would draw, or paint, or sculpt clay together as group members took turns reading the tales. In one instance, a fourteen-year-old, acting-out patient sculpted a clay piece of two figures, a male and a female, joined together at the feet, after listening to a fairy tale. When it was his turn to talk about his work, he said, "This is my mother and me joined together, and we can't get apart." The story and the art together seemed to facilitate the young man's expression of his symbiotic relationship with his mother, shown unmistakably in the clay. Neither mother nor son could move or function until they individuated as separate beings.

In other settings as well, fairy tales can be used to help people discover the archetypal patterns that influence their lives. With whom, they might ask themselves, do they identify? The hero? The victim? The witch? How about other important figures in their lives? Do they see their parents as mean ogres, or their mate or children as actors in a fairy tale drama?

The art work, too, often brings up long-forgotten childhood memories, or family-of-origin patterns of interaction, or patterns of behavior that listeners may have established unconsciously as adults. As the student, patient, or client listens to the story, the art is used to depict aspects of the story that are of particular interest or attract their attention. After the art work is completed, the work is processed, or discussed, in relation to events in their lives.

Back to our fairy tale, *The Magic Swan Geese.* This tale was used as a catalyst for workshop members to relate to during a recent weekend intensive facilitated by the authors. One of the group members, Margie, was especially intrigued by the art work that she completed in the group.

Margie responded to her poster in two phases: her first response was during the weekend intensive, the second was during an individual therapy session. We scheduled another individual session for Margie to talk about the two phases of the processing of her picture. Corbit is the therapist.

Phase I:

Margie: I initially wanted my picture to represent the cakras. That's what this rainbow is, my inner life. As I built the cakras, I realized that there's always a dark side to the bright side, so that's why I put the dark area in—to represent the negative force that propels us. Because I believe that there is light in the dark, that's the reason I put the sparkles in. And I was running from the dark side over here with the bundle that would represent my smaller self running from the dark side.
So can you associate that to the fairy tale? Is that running away from Baba Yaga?
Margie: Umhumm. Trying to escape.
So Baba Yaga would have represented a lot more in your life.

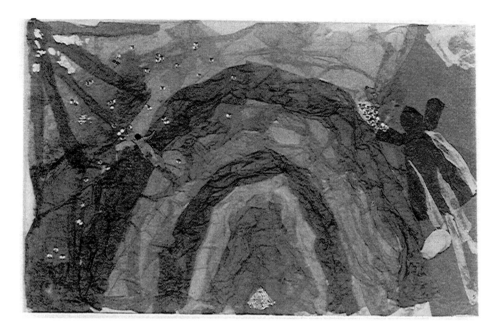

Figure 5-1. Margie's poster done in response to the fairy tale, "The Magic Swan Geese."

Margie: Yes. It represented those negative forces, those negative things that have chased me.

And that you have possibly kept in the unconscious.

Margie: Umhumm. You see, I believe that this propelled me to where I am now, that the benefit of this negative side is the positive side that I am today.

Yes, because you have to look at that negative side and accept it.

Margie: Absolutely, absolutely. And so it has given me the strength, the drive to find a spiritual life that's satisfying to me. Everything about my life that I find as satisfying today is the result of the negative forces as well as the positive force. And the positive force I felt like is inside of me, and this was the outside force, this negative was the outside force that has made me come into my own. And so, in this figure, I'm running . . .

Running, almost flying.

Margie: Yes, it almost looks like I'm flying to the light. This is done now. Although this will always be here, this negative side, will always be here with the light energy, but it propels me toward the light.

Also, something that I hadn't noticed before was, over there the light, those little sparkles are all in one place, and over here they are dispersed all over.

Margie: Because that's all of this glitters, glistens. It's really fun to stay over here, this is the way out.

Now is that in the hand of the "dark force?"

Margie: Umhumm. And to me that represented the good that is inside the evil. And this is my center, my core, the part of God that is Margie, and it sits in the middle.

Phase II:

O.K. I can recall more clearly now the session that you and I had about "the force" (a recent therapy session), but why don't you tell me your story again.

Margie: About the "near death" experience? I was in the hospital. I had spinal meningitis *and* St. Louis encephalitis. I was dying. I had been in and out of coma for days. I had asked for my parish priest to come and give me the last rites. And he had declined, saying since I was in a Catholic hospital, I could use the services of the chaplain there. Made me angry. It's part of what saved my life, I think. So this one day, I was lying in my hospital bed. It was broad daylight. I had opened my eyes to where I looked at the door. And, as I looked at the door, this figure appeared, this shrouded figure appeared who looked like a monk with a hood over what would be his face, but there was no face. And he raised up his arm with his hand, and had there been a hand it would have been outstretched, but there was no hand, it was just the robes. And I heard him say inside my head, not outside my head, that it's like I knew this figure was speaking to me. It was awesome. I wasn't afraid at all. I was in awe of this "being." There was that kind of energy about it, and he said, "It's time for you to come with me."

And I lay there, and I knew that he had come to get me, so that I could die. And I thought about the three children that I had, and who would raise them? I thought about their growing up with Jim's parents or them growing up with my parents or them growing up with Jim alone. And by then Jim was an alcoholic; his alcoholism was already destructive to the family. And so I saw that I was the one that had to influence my own children, that I wouldn't be happy with somebody else doing that. And so I said, "No! I won't go." And I wasn't angry, I just said, "No!"

As if to say, "No, it's not time."

Margie: It was actually very conversational-like. And he stood there for a while with his hand outstretched and we looked at each other, and then he faded. His robes were gray, deep, deep gray to almost black. Maybe it was the lighting in the room, I don't know what it was. And I can feel that "presence" just right now. When I tell the story, it always brings me the chills. I don't tell the story very often, but when I tell the story that "presence" always comes with the story to be here. And then I get a sense in the now, that my path is lighted.

A real sense of spirit.

Margie: And every time I light that spirit, that "being," with the telling of that story, that's the sense that I get.

So, I guess that your artwork brought all of this up again. Even though it seems to be a dark spirit, and possibly even somewhat evil, it still is very humbling. It holds the balance of the opposites. It just is. It's life and it's death. And who's to say is life right and death wrong?

Margie: It's neither good nor evil. It's the balance.
Tremendous power! Even in the picture, look how much larger that figure is than the ones of you.
Margie: And you know when I put this one up, when I constructed this picture, this was an afterthought. I had the brown to represent the dark, and the "being" came almost last. It just had to be there.
But you didn't have in mind the "near death" experience?
Margie: No. Not a bit, not a bit. It wasn't until we were here in your office again that I remembered it.
I think that we had mentioned something about an archangel.
Margie: Yes. And then I remembered it. And so this "being" has been ... maybe that is part of why so much has happened to me, but I'm not destroyed. Because I feel that "being" has been really close to me all along.
And, you know that there's no guarantee that a lot of negative things won't happen. I mean, life being what it is, there are always lots of negative things to happen. But, nevertheless, you now have, at least symbolically, a clue to an inward guide, or a spiritual guide.
Margie: It's never far away, if I remember it. It's the remembering ...
Umhumm.
Margie: This spirit, I know, has guided this path, this heart that's my artwork. I look at some of it, especially the beginning stuff—those first pictures that I did (in residential treatment) when I was starting to get my story. And it seemed like such an unbelievable story. And it seems so unbelievable because of the condition that I'm in today ... So, I know the feeling that I get when I'm in this "presence," now that I can recognize it. That was the feeling that a lot of those pictures were drawn with (during residential treatment). That energy was about me. I would sit at the lunch time, we didn't have any free time, really, only an hour between lunch and the next session. And so I would go back to the lecture place and get out the art material and put on a meditation tape and just sit there by myself and do those pictures. Then I know the influence was there, because I feel truth with this energy. And no matter how awful it appeared to be, it was the truth, it wasn't a made up story. And then it's over. So, I feel like that's grace.
That sounds so. It's almost like being in limbo, isn't it? Like being in suspension. And that's where you were with death calling, you were in suspension because you were so close.
Margie: All I had to do was say "Yes." All I had to do was reach out my hand, Irene, I didn't have to even say yes.

Margie processed her art work which she created in response to the fairy tale in two separate phases, on two different levels. In the first phase, the level of the personal unconscious, Margie was able to relate to the girl running from the bad witch, Baba Yaga. Margie, too, ever since childhood had been running from negative forces which had been hurtful to her. For years she had buried painful memories until they began intruding upon her consciousness, disrupting her successful business life, and eventually forcing her to seek treatment.

In the second phase, Margie began to associate the dark figure in her poster to memories of a messenger of death who had visited her when she was critically ill. Incidentally, Margie did not purposely compose this figure of death in her artwork. She had, in fact, at first seen the figure as a dark hand. This image of death, which Margie identified and associated to in her art poster, might be termed "The Archetype of Death."

This Archetype of Death is mentioned in von Franz's book *Shadow and evil in fairytales* (1974) in which she describes the witch Baba Yaga as the great Mother Nature:

> She could not talk about "My day, My night!" if she were not the owner of the day, of the night, and of the sun, so she must be a great Goddess and you could call her the Great Goddess of Nature. Obviously, with all those skulls around her hut, she is also the Goddess of Death, which is an aspect of nature . . . So she is a Goddess of day and night, of life and death, and the great principle of nature (pp. 161–162).

Interestingly, Margie had no prior knowledge of Baba Yaga and her dual roles as the Great Goddess of Nature and the Goddess of Death, yet in response to this fairy tale, with Baba Yaga playing a featured role, Margie created a rainbow, the sun (prominent in her description of her work, to which she ran or flew), and the Archangel of Death.

"So what?" you might ask, "of what help is it to draw pictures and to discover one's active archetypes?"

For Margie, this new awareness and knowledge of these active archetypes begins to give her a better understanding of herself, her behavior, and her interactions with others. The better we understand the archetypes within ourselves, the more we can participate in the collective life and realize the timelessness of humanity as revealed in the archetypes. Margie now is beginning to recognize more of the things in life that make her feel good and make her feel bad. She honors herself as a nature worshipper. She feels in harmony with the out of doors: at the seashore, in the woods, on the desert, anywhere that she is in direct contact with nature. Margie's inner work, too, has helped her to become more in touch with her own wants and needs. Feelings that were buried because of the pain connected with them are gradually being examined and acknowledged. Finally, through engaging with the archetype of Death, Margie is beginning to experience life.

This might be the time to go to Jung (Collected Works, Vol 9) for his definition of the collective unconscious:

> The collective unconscious is a part of the psyche which can be negatively distinguished from a personal unconscious by the fact that it does not, like the latter, owe its existence to personal experience and consequently is not a personal acquisition. While the personal unconscious is made up essentially of contents which have at one time been conscious but which have disappeared from consciousness through having been forgotten or depressed, the contents of the collective unconscious have never been in consciousness, and therefore have never been individually acquired, but owe their existence exclusively to heredity. Whereas the personal unconscious consists for the most part of *complexes,* the content of the collective unconscious is made up essentially of *archetypes* (pp. 42–43).

Edinger (1972) believed the collective unconscious to be Jung's most basic and far-reaching discovery. He pointed out that the collective unconscious has a transpersonal dimension that can be recognized in all the world's religions and myths. Edinger credited Jung with the important discovery, too, that the collective unconscious has a dynamic quality in that it provides a structuring or ordering principle that unifies the contents of the archetypes. That is, the structure or organization of the collective unconscious is itself an archetype, the archetype of the Self.

Jung (Collected Works, Vol. 7) describes the unconscious as containing two layers, the personal and the collective. The personal unconscious is similar to Freud's concept of the unconscious that is made up of repressed memories of early infancy. The collective unconscious predates the individual and contains residues of ancestral life. The archetypes of the collective unconscious are not personally experienced so they are not detailed, completed cores, but are rather one-dimensional forms. It is possible for one to come in contact with these archetypal motifs when the psyche regresses beyond the level of the personal unconscious.

Margie's reaction to the archetypal images in the fairy tale, *The Magic Swan Geese,* is not uncommon. These very basic fairy tale motifs of risk-taking, betrayal, death, and chicanery are all a part of the human condition which affect every one of us.

Elizabeth's associations to the same fairy tale, *The Magic Swan Geese,* were very different from Margie's. Elizabeth chose a piece of black poster board for her background. The scene that she depicted from the story was of the imposing figure of Baba Yaga peering around the mountain in pursuit of a fleeing girl.

Figure 5-2. An illustration by Elizabeth of "The Magic Swan Geese."

In describing her artwork, Elizabeth recalled her unhappy childhood relationship with her mother in which she always felt like the "bad little girl," rarely receiving her mother's approval. As she grew up, this early shadow relationship with her mother was reenacted many times over with other women she perceived to be negative who played influential roles in her life. This basic pattern of behavior continued until Elizabeth began to see the similarities in these relationships and her need to confront and remedy her interactions with powerful women.

From an historical perspective, Elizabeth talked about her own mother also suffering from a negative mother relationship. When Elizabeth's mother was only ten years old, *her* mother died, leaving her to be reared by a critical, nonapproving stepmother.

The importance of Elizabeth's work, of course, is not only to heal her own interactions with women she perceived to be negative, but to end the female legacy in her family by not, in turn, becoming a powerful negative female figure, another Baba Yaga. This Baba Yaga archetype, or archetype of the negative female, might be recognized in dreams, fairy tales, myths, and active imagination in the forms of the Medusa, the witch, the wicked stepmother, the crone, or the temptress.

Elizabeth, herself, recalls a shadow dream in which an obese woman dressed in black became the leading figure in the dream. They were returning from Galveston. Elizabeth was driving. The day was hot. The woman in black was in the back seat of the car with her own child; several other children were also in the car. The woman asked Elizabeth to pull up and stop at a convenience store. She went into the store leaving Elizabeth behind with a car full of hot and sweaty children. The woman in black returned licking on an ice cream cone, not once considering the other hot and hungry occupants of the car.

Elizabeth was reluctant to believe that the obese woman in black, that self-gratifying woman could be any part of her. It certainly was not a part of herself that she recognized, nor did she want to accept it as a part of her personality. For many, this assimilation of shadow figures is slow and painful. In Elizabeth's case, she began to see that there was a part of herself that needed attention and nurturing. Who loves a sweaty fat woman? Who wants to relate to someone who is so selfish, so narcissistic? But this painful process of integration is a major part of Jung's individuation process, of developing our personality to its fullest—accepting and transforming those shadow parts, both the positive and the negative.

Jung (Collected Works, Vol. 9, Pt. 1) felt that myths and fairy tales were well-known expressions of the archetypes. He saw archetypes as psychic contents which have not been brought to consciousness nor undergone conscious elaboration. The immediate manifestation of this archetypal material, for example, dream contents or visions, is much more individual, less naive, and less understandable than archetypal material found in myths and fairy tales. In other words, archetypal material in myths (or fairy tales) is more easily identified, then worked through on a psychological level. "The archetype," Jung says (p. 5), "is essentially an unconscious content that is altered by becoming conscious and by being perceived, and it takes its color from the individual consciousness in which it happens to appear."

Now hear about Mizilca.

Mizilca (Seemann, Stromback, and Jonsson, 1967, pp. 170–181) is a

Romanian ballad believed to be based upon a common theme in traditional European fairy tales and songs: that of a girl who disguises herself
as a man and goes off to the wars in the place of her father. According to
the story, Mizilca's father, King Mizil, is ordered by the Sultan to send a
son to bear arms for the Sultan for a period of seven and a half years. But
because the King had no sons, only three healthy daughters, he was
unable to obey the Sultan's command.

When the King read the Sultan's words, he became grief-stricken and
filled with fear. He wept and groaned until his daughters became quite
concerned about his health. When the King's oldest daughter, Stanuta,
heard about her father's plight, she volunteered to take his place. She
had her hair cut short, was equipped with the finest horse and soldier's
clothing, and set out to serve the Sultan. But the King, using his magic
(for he was also a magician), decided to test the girl. He turned himself
into a dragon, which filled Stanuta with such fear and awe that she
turned back to her father's palace.

Next the King's daughter, Roxanda, volunteered to serve the Sultan in
the place of her father. She, too, had her hair cut short in a soldier's style,
was outfitted in the clothes of a hero, and was given one of her father's
finest horses. But, alas, the King again turned himself into a dragon and
frightened Roxanda so badly that she, too, turned in her tracks and fled
back to her father's palace.

Next, the King's youngest daughter, Mizilca, pleaded with her father
to allow her to serve the Sultan since he had no son to serve. "Let
me cut my hair as the soldiers do and have the clothes that the heroes
wear," she said. When Mizilca went to select a horse (and he offered her
the finest of his horses), she first chose a bridle from the King's early
days as a soldier. She then hit the bridle on the ground to call one of the
King's horses. The horse that came to her was the weakest horse in the
stable. Again she hit the bridle on the ground, and again this same weak
horse came to her feet. When after the third time she hit the bridle to the
ground and the weak horse came to her, she accepted the horse as the one
to take.

As with the King's other two daughters, King Mizil tested Mizilca's
courage as he turned himself into a bold dragon. But Mizilca was not to
be frightened! She challenged the magical dragon that he placed in her
path, and went on to serve her time at the Sultan's palace.

Once Mizilca arrived at the Sultan's palace, he looked her up and
down, frowned, and said:

> Look, the Devil's mother, plain to see,
> See herself presented has to me.
> What I see can hero hardly ape,
> 'Tis assuredly a woman's shape.

The Sultan became obsessed to learn Mizilca's true sexual identity. He had one of his guardsmen take Mizilca to the market, where on one side were distaffs used in weaving fabrics. On the other side were clubs. Mizilca, alert to the Sultan's trickery, chose a heavy club which she flung into the air and out of sight. The Sultan was so impressed by her feat that he appointed her to be an officer.

As time went by, the Sultan again was plagued by his doubts. He instructed a guardsman to fetch Mizilca and take her to the bathing place. The guardsman was to watch as Mizilca bathed and he was to observe whether or not she had breasts. Mizilca, realizing that she was soon to be discovered, buttoned, then unbuttoned her shirt as the guardsman swam to and fro. Finally, Mizilca came up with an idea: a letter. The letter said that her mother had died and was now on the funeral pyre. She must return home, so said the urgent letter.

When the Sultan read the letter, he at once commanded Mizilca to return home. Without ado, Mizilca swung onto her horse, dug the spurs in, then turned and opened wide her blouse, displaying her breasts for all to see. Then she called out to the Sultan:

> High and might ruler, praised be!
> I know more of you than you of me,
> Aye, although I but a maiden be.

Then, so saying, she turned, spurred her horse, and started on her way. Her steed then spread six pairs of wings and, as if on sunbeams, she sped to her father's castle and home.

The archetypal theme of the next poster might be called "androgyny." Androgyny or androgyne, according to *A Critical Dictionary of Jungian Analysis* (Samuels, Shorter and Plaut, 1986), is a

Psychic PERSONIFICATION which holds male and female in conscious balance. In this figure the principles of male and female are conjoined without merger of characteristics. It was this metaphorical being and not the undifferentiated HERMAPHRODITE that Jung saw as symbolizing the end product of the alchemical process. The IMAGE of the androgyne is, therefore, relevant to ANALYSIS, most especially in relation to work with ANIMA AND ANIMUS. In alchemical treatises there are not only references but frequent illustrations of this figure. More than once, Jung drew attention to the historical person of Jesus as an example of one in whom the tension and polarity of SEXUAL DIFFERENTIATION has been resolved in androgynous complementarity and unity (p. 22).

Singer (1976, p. 20) defines androgyny as "the One which contains the Two." The One is identified as the male (andro) and the Two means the female (gyne). Singer says that androgyny "is an archetype *inherent in the human psyche.*"

Singer continues (p. 21) that the one pair, which includes male and female, represents the symbolic expression of the energetic power behind all of the other polarities. As creating principles, one is invalid without the other. Male and female must join together in the wholeness of their sexuality for creation to be engendered. But before they can be joined, they must first become separated, differentiated beings. This suggests Plato's image of the primal androgyne, bound together in one sphere.

Our current knowledge regarding the primal qualities of the androgyne, Singer says (p. 21), comes from remnants found in myths and legends and sacred traditions of many primitive peoples. She cites ancient mythology for the tales of a time when the "eternal male and the eternal female were locked in an unending embrace." Singer sees that this androgynous primal being, containing within itself the potentialities of duality and multiplicity, has filtered down to us through knowledge of many religions, including Hinduism, Taoism, and Buddhism, as well as "Platonic traditions of religions of the West."

Bradway (1982) writes of the way in which expectations for men and women have changed recently through more of an appreciation of the androgyny. She sees androgyny as a means for overcoming stereotypical attitudes regarding appropriate behavior for males and females. One then has the possibility of developing a more flexible behavior for particular situations, more assertive or aggressive in certain instances, and more caring or nurturing when that is required.

The archetype of the androgyny, which carries aspects of both the male and the female, can be viewed as a symbol of wholeness, the bringing together of the opposites. In alchemy, the androgyne was depicted as the hermaphrodite, the half man, half woman figure, but Bradway states that "Jung saw the symbol of the hermaphrodite as tending to break down into its components, thus turning into a symbol representing potential dissociation. Jung would have seen the symbol of *coniunctio* as offering a more stable symbol than the hermaphrodite or androgyne in the formation of wholeness" (Bradway, p. 282).

"To me," Bradway says, "androgyny represents dual attitudes and behavior at a conscious level, whereas the *coniunctio* represents the coming together—the 'marriage'—of the masculine and feminine principles at an unconscious level. Androgyny seems to have to do with role, *coniunctio* with identity" (p. 282).

This dual attitude regarding the masculine and feminine principles is paramount in the story of Mizilca. Mizilca knew that to save her father she must masquerade as a young man. When her father turned himself into a dragon, Mizilca did not run in fear, but faced the dragon head on. She was cunning enough not to fall for the tricks designed by the Sultan when he attempted to discover whether Mizilca was a maiden or a lad. When the time was ripe, Mizilca was, indeed, bold enough to let the Sultan know her gender by baring her breasts as she left his palace gates.

Our next poster was composed by Liz, a mature woman intently interested in creativity, self-discovery, and continuing education. On her personal journey, Liz created a series of fairy tale posters, including two depicting the story of Mizilca. This is the second of her Mizilca series.

In describing her Mizilca poster, Liz says:

Figure 5-3. One of a series of illustrations done by Liz, in response to the story of "Mizilca."

I show her leaving the Sultan, bare-breasted and riding a saggy-backed horse. I show her images as internal and external facing in many directions, finally standing on the "steps of learning" with a briefcase in hand. Does she know what she will do? She knows she had a good expansive year with the Sultan. She'll probably go back to her father's castle. She'll love her father for trying to protect her and her sisters who were brave before her. I have a sense she is aware and knows she has choices as a woman. Maybe she'll become a Sultan.

Fairy tales and myths have been excellent themes for me to use in art therapy. These stories help my unconscious to come closer to awareness. Art therapy enriches my verbal psychotherapy. These fantasy tales provoke me at a different level. For me, art is physically therapeutic. I let go of tension when I am working with the materials. At times my finished product can seem clumsy and inarticulate. Many times I will use my less dominant hand or close my eyes to keep from thinking as I do my art creations. I want to know what is going on deep inside me and in some subliminal way that takes place through art. Harriet Wadeson describes art therapy as a "doing" therapy. You create your own artwork. No priest or priestess is going to come and zap you with a wand. The process is experiential and you are in charge of the process. Similarly if a woman is going to write her life beyond "living happily ever after," she is going to have to seek and respond in an active way. She must stay constantly challenged. I find that by looking at the fantasy in my life and taking those images into creative art, facilitated by a therapist, I am a more confident centered woman.

Here is a verbatim excerpt from the therapy session focused on the artwork pictured in Figure 5-3, above. The therapist is Corbit:

Liz: I can remember being fascinated by the Sultan. And I didn't want her to go home and live happily ever after. I wanted her to go home and reunite with her family and then be brave enough to go on and do something that she really wanted to do.

That's a good piece of information.

Liz: I did not want her to live happily ever after, really, from the way we look at fairy tales. I wanted something different to happen to her, and, of course, this is the Sultan, which, I guess, I liked his role in the fairy tale because I had no idea what he would have done if he found out she was a lass. But he seemed curious and not cruel or vindictive.

He didn't post anybody to spy on her, which he could easily have done.

Liz: So I had a good feeling about him. I guess that I thought he was a good male image for her. And I loved the bare breast—that's *my* bared breast. That was exciting for me. And then I began to realize that she would have to go through many changes. The other thing I remember is that I also was clear that if her first sister had not had enough courage to go, even if it was just as far as the bridge, and if her second sister hadn't had enough courage to go, even though it was to the bridge, I'm not sure Mizilca could have done that. Or if she could do it herself, how successful she would have been. They were supportive even though it wasn't discussed. They gave her the image of courage.

So you think the other two girls supported her cause? Were these three images here the three sisters?

Liz: Yes. Symbolically. Because it can almost be the stages she went through. And I was thinking of myself because what is art therapy for if you don't do that through circumstances? And so I was wondering at the same time what opportunities I had at that time. And when I left the room to have the Polaroid® pictures taken with two associates, I took Jerry's briefcase ... it isn't really a briefcase. It's kind of old and thin. It's exactly what I wanted. To be able to wear that and put it on and do what I needed to do whether it was to go on to school, because I'd had them take this picture on the stairs going into the school, made me feel like a sophomore, made me feel as though I had taken some of the wisdom from the fairy tales and used it for myself. I guess for one thing I'm really aware of working on the masculine within myself and how I am able to get that to be a powerful support model.

And for years you've worked on yourself in attempting to get to know yourself and be assertive and to really get in touch with all of the different aspects of what you're about.

Liz: And, of course, I really believe the story of Mizilca brought that home to me in a big way. It's a wonderful fairy tale, but it's me. I'm the Sultan and the princess and even the old father, I guess.

There wasn't any young prince in the story or anybody that she had to marry. In most fairy tales the young maiden gets her reward at the end by getting to marry a prince and this tale didn't have anything like that.

Liz: I guess this is why ... what you just said is why I started looking at the Sultan being a part of the positive male image in the story, and it would not have surprised me for her to have ended up marrying him. And that did not happen. And then I had to start looking around for that other male.

And yet for Mizilca, what I see is that she had this androgyny where she didn't really need a male model. She was able to accept both the male and the female parts of herself.

Liz: Yes, and that's what came through so clear to me, using what I thought a Sultan would learn of this ... and the bared breast. I think that's what I decided upon that she didn't need anybody else, that she had it all. She didn't have to have somebody come in and marry her to make her happy.

After you did this, or even right at this point, do you sense more of the male and female roles within yourself after using this fairy tale as an example?

Liz: Oh, yes, very definitely! You know I had forgotten so much because it's been several months, but from our discussion, discussing it here today, I won't be surprised if I don't do a third one. And at this minute I really don't know how I would do it. But it's made me look at bringing all the male and female together with the inside, and not being afraid of it. I guess for me I always felt too aggressive or too assertive.

And what Mizilca did, she did things like men because she posed as a man for a time, and yet she was still proud of being a woman. And so there, to me, was this real sense of androgyny.

Liz: Very definitely.
But she's not going to go back home and play the role of a man, she's going to go back and be a girl.

In our follow-up interview, Liz gained more perspective on her work with her Mizilca posters. From the first time that she heard the fairy tale, Liz was fascinated with the story, a reaction common to people who relate to a fairy tale on an archetypal level. In Liz's case, this ability to switch roles struck a chord very deep within her. Later in our interview, Liz relayed how important she felt it was for women to be able to use a screwdriver and to fix and repair things, and not assigning these duties to a man. She was empathetic with the Sultan. Although he was a powerful man, nevertheless, he was just a man. He sought the advice of the wise woman and used the feminine ploys of manipulation and trickery in attempts to discover Mizilca's gender, but did not use the more masculine methods of force or invasive techniques.

Liz, too, was amused at Mizilca's somewhat brazen behavior in baring her breasts to the Sultan to prove her womanhood. Her desire to see Mizilca "be brave enough to go on and do something that she really wanted to do" carries the fairy tale past the end of the tale and into the realm of active imagination. In her poster, Liz, as Mizilca, poses herself on the steps of the university going back to school, an action which to her was intimidating, yet adventurous. Fairy tales are symbolic representations of human problems and of possible solutions to these problems, so, in identifying with Mizilca and her risk-taking behavior, Liz can now give herself permission to achieve an unfulfilled dream and complete her degree.

Androgyny, which in Jung's day was more of a perceived model than a fact of life, is becoming a reality in today's world. The women's movement, which began almost two decades ago, helped women to find their androgynous roles in society. Women began to move out of their earlier locked-in roles and insisted upon roles more satisfying to them. Civil rights legislation was passed which provided access to areas that previously were male sanctuaries. Conversely, areas that were totally female strongholds are becoming options for men. Men all over the country now are developing their own movement. In gathering together, they get in touch with their own androgynous nature, which includes expressing feelings, relating to other men, and drumming (possibly taking them back to that beat of their mother's heart).

As most of us have observed, this social shift has begun to create changes in life styles, in the work place, and in relationships. We might wonder at this point whether the shift has come from pressures within the environment or from a deep-seated archetypal need which is at last being identified and actualized. Androgyny does not preclude being a mother, a wife, a nurturer, a husband, a father, or a provider, but it does open doors for both sexes to enjoy their archetypal and androgynous natures.

Chapter 6

DREAMS AND ACTIVE IMAGINATION

What do our dreams tell us? Are they remnants of the previous day's happenings? Can they be considered the brain's way of cleaning house or erasing useless or nonsensical memories, as proposed by Crick and Mitchison (Melnechuk, 1983)? Or, can it be that they convey messages from God (Kelsey, 1978)?

We believe dreams and nightmares to be many things: They provide insights to otherwise opaque understandings of self, they expand consciousness, they resolve problems, both physical and mental, they relieve stress, they complement the psyche, and, furthermore, they provide a rich source of creativity.

Freud was the first of the modern pioneers in psychology who attempted to explore empirically the unconscious background of consciousness. Freud thought of dreams as vehicles for the expression of unconscious impulses. The idea is that, during sleep, wishes that have been repressed are able to be expressed because censoring forces that are present during the waking state are relaxed during sleep, and the wishes are allowed into consciousness, although in disguised form. The wishes are disguised in order to protect the sleep of the dreamer. The wishes, in undisguised form, would create anxiety and disturb the dreamer. The dream, as it is literally told, was considered by Freud to be a *manifest* facade. The facade conceals the inner, or *latent,* meaning of the dream which he thought of as some form of forbidden wish.

In Freud's therapy the dreamer free associates his dream images and thoughts through a train of ideas and the psychoanalyst analyzes the wish fulfillment and repression evident in the latent content. Dreams are not a matter of chance, Freud speculated, but are associated with conscious and unconscious thoughts and problems, and through dreams neurotic symptoms can be resolved. These symptoms, he felt, were related to some conscious experience. In Freud's method of free association the dreamer is encouraged to continue to talk about his dream images and the thoughts that these prompt in his mind. In this way he will give himself away and reveal the unconscious background of his neurosis, both by what he says and what he does not say.

In contrast, Jung's analytic therapy suggests that the dreamer stay as close as possible to the dream content, focusing on the associations to the dream itself. The dreamer is to exclude all irrelevant ideas and associations that the dream might evoke. Jung says that "while 'free' association lures one away from that material in a kind of a zigzag line, the method I evolved is more like a circumambulation whose center is the dream picture. I work all around the dream picture and disregard every attempt that the dreamer makes to break away from it" (1964, p. 29).

Jung's method encourages the dreamer to amplify the association of specific aspects of his dream to discover elements missing from his conscious viewpoint. In the amplification of the associations, analogous material from myth and fantasy will often emerge to help illuminate the dream symbolism (Singer, 1972). Through the dream, the unconscious strives to bring balance to the psyche by completing, enlarging, or compensating the conscious attitude. Disowned or missing elements of which the ego is unaware are thus brought to conscious awareness.

Jung also made the point that dreams often contain impressions and "unfinished business" from the day's events. Even so, Jung saw dreams to be much more than a mechanism for detailing impressions from the previous day. He saw dreams as compensatory to current conscious situations. The dreams act as a self-regulating aspect of the psyche. The conscious attitude often is one-sided, leading a person to deviate from an optimal way of life. The dream tends to compensate for this one-sided consciousness by emphasizing the opposite attitude. In extreme instances, when a person is overly rigid in her conscious life, the dreams will be startlingly powerful reminders of that rigidity is a warning to her that her vital needs are being neglected.

Jung felt that there are two ways in which the dream can be approached: The first is the objective approach which explores each character in the dream as a person in the real world, as relationships, as real life situations. The dream provides a view on relational or situational happenings in the real world which have remained conscious to the dreamer. From this perspective, the dream might present a solution to an imbalance or out-of-adjustment situation in the dreamer's life. Jung stressed the importance of bringing harmony to the opposites in the psyche.

The second method of working on dreams is the subjective approach. On the subjective level the dreamer views all persons in the dream as being aspects of her personality. People unknown to the dreamer or people in the dreamer's waking life, but not of current concern, can be interpreted as personifications of archetypal aspects of oneself. Both points of view need to be considered, with a possible bias toward the subjective.

Just as in fairy tales and myths, many dreams also contain archetypal images. These dreams might be considered "big" dreams, says Hall (1982, p. 136), "touching upon the characterological structure of the personality and having a valid meaning over months or years." Hall continues, "All such dreams can be considered symbolic statements, but some reach even the archetypal level of symbolization, using images that are meaningful in mythological or religious systems that may not even be known to the dreamer's waking mind."

The archetypal dream carries healing and transformational power. This archetypal dream might present unworldly images to the dreamer, such as images of giants, dwarfs, precocious infants, or animals that talk. Clients and students often report that they experience a numinous feeling which lingers long after the archetypal dream. When a client or student has had such a dream which carries great affect with it, we ask her not to attempt to interpret the dream or to take it apart, but to simply draw the dream and "live with" the images and the feelings. In our experience, the dreamer who is willing to simply "live with" the images and the feelings, discovers that the dream continues to affect her and to present new material both in her inner world and her outer world for some time to come. Even in the case of a so-called "bad" dream which might contain archetypal contents, we have found that "living with" and befriending the dream brings about its own resolutions.

This method of honoring the images is based upon the archetypal psychology work of James Hillman. He says (1975):

> We sin against the imagination whenever we ask an image for its meaning, requiring that images be translated into concepts. The coiled snake in the corner cannot be translated into my fear, my sexuality, or my mother-complex without killing the snake. We do not hear music, touch sculpture, or read stories with meaning in mind, but for the sake of the imagination. Though art may hide a multitude of psychological ignorances, at least it does not ask images what they mean. Interpretations and even amplifications of images, including the whole analytical kit of symbolic dictionaries and ethnological parallels, too often become instruments of allegory. Rather than vivifying the imagination by connecting our conceptual intellects with the images of dreams and fantasies, they exchange the image for a commentary on it or digest of it.

And these interpretations forget too that they are themselves fantasies induced by the image, no more meaningful than the image itself. (p. 40)

Unlike Freud, Jung wanted his patients to work with their own dreams, rather than to rely on analysis by the therapist. He cautioned that the analyst's interpretation must be tentative until confirmed by the patient. Singer (1972, p. 276) says that "The whole point of dream analysis is to teach the patient eventually to become independent of the therapist, by acquiring the ability to carry on the dialogue with his own inner aspect which has a therapeutic quality, that is, with 'the therapist within.' "

Jung often suggested that his clients paint or draw their dreams, a way in which to amplify their dream material. In workshops and in classes, we also encourage students and clients to enhance their dreams using art and photography. The dream takes on new meaning, new dimensions when aspects of the dream are depicted in clay, collage, paints, oil pastels, or photography. At one level, the dream often gives a succinct message that appears to be clear and brief and understandable. Then, as we look at the dream from a more subjective level, using the artwork, it presents a totally different meaning.

How do we work with a dream that is presented to us? Dreams, of course, can be explored from various theoretical viewpoints. Jung's basic method of working with dreams would likely be our first choice when a dream is presented. Or, if the client or student presents a dream rich in numinous archetypal material, we might ask the client or student to paint the dream, to sculpt some aspect of it, to use photography depicting their role in the dream, or to create a collage which represents the dream or the feeling-tone of the dream. The individual then, using Hillman's archetypal method, would validate the images. "We learn from the alchemical psychologists to let the image work upon the experimenter," Hillman says (1975, p. 40), "we learn to become the object of the work— even an object, or objectified image of the imagination."

McNiff (1990, p. 27) considers archetypal psychology to be a theory "that derives from images and attends to the sensory and psychic qualities of images. Rather than using the image and information provided by the senses as 'raw material' for rational analysis, archetypal psychology strives to let images illuminate consciousness." He agrees with Hillman's concept that fantasy work is closely related to the arts, such as writing, music and painting. When working and playing with one's imagination, the strength of the internal images waxes while the strength of the ego wanes.

If the client or student comes to a session or a class with a nightmare, we might consider using the Malaysian Senoi people's method of working with dreams. Over the years, we have found this method to be extremely beneficial when working with children's nightmares or adults' nightmares or nightmares that adults have had as children. To begin the work, we ask that clients or students draw the nightmare as they remember it. Next, they may wish to have their dream image captured in photography so that, in essence, they can actually become a part of their dream picture. At this point, we follow Johnston's techniques that he has developed based on Senoi philosophy (1978). Johnston suggests that the leader begin the process by telling the dreamer to "close your eyes and let me know when you are in the dream." After the dreamer acknowledges that he is back into the dream, the leader then asks, "What is happening now?" The dreamer is led through six stages in this dream process which Johnston has labeled Key, Embellishment, Main Figure, Gift, Artifact, and Quest.

First, the dreamer is asked to find the fundamental essence of the dream, what Johnston called the Key. The essence of the dream may be a brief image, a feeling, a color, a person or animal in the dream. For example, the dreamer may say that the dream did not make much sense, but the essence of it was that it was frightening. The key to the dream is the emotion of fear. The essence of the dream is called the key because it can unlock, can lead to the rest of the dream, even if the dream seems to be unfinished. The key allows the dreamer to get back into the dream, as much as possible in the waking state.

The Embellishment phase begins when the dreamer is actively recalling or reliving the dream. He recites the dream aloud in first person, present tense. The leader might assist by asking leading questions of the dreamer regarding site, environment, sounds, or feelings. As the dreamer embellishes the key essence of the dream, the Main Figure often emerges. The main figure can be a human, a monster, an animal, or even an amorphous shape.

The dreamer next attempts to engage the main figure in dialogue. If the main figure appears to be frightening or violent, the dreamer may then muster allies to come to his aid. The dreamer must, first and foremost, be comfortable enough with the main figure to relate to it in some way. This may mean creating some imaginary distance between himself and the main figure. If the main figure becomes hostile, the dreamer can ask, "How may I help you?" If the main figure is reluctant to answer, the dreamer can persist or rephrase the question.

The third stage is a time for exchanging gifts between the dreamer and the main figure. The gift is a symbol of alliance between the main figure and the dreamer. At this stage, the dreamer simply imagines the forms of the gifts.

During the next phase, the dreamer creates the gifts that will be exchanged with the main figure, in some tangible form. He can first sketch or otherwise make preliminary outlines of the gifts, then sculpt, paint, write or somehow fashion the gifts. He then imagines the interchange of gifts with the main figure.

The Quest is the time when the participant can search in the waking world for the images representative of the gifts. The quest may take a few minutes or several days. The dreamer may have only a vague idea of the form of the gifts, but will recognize them when he sees them. Johnston sees this quest as symbolizing the search for an internal spiritual goal, as well as for its symbolic counterpart in the real world.

When using this method with children's nightmares, we sometimes use an abbreviated form. The child first draws the nightmare or uses photography to put himself into the bad dream. Often the child tells the nightmare as he is doing his artwork. Next, we ask the child to find some allies to take back into the nightmare. He might command the police force or the army or even his pet to come back into his dream to protect him. First and foremost, the child *must* feel absolutely safe before reentering the dream. The child is then directed to speak to the nightmare figure; the tiger or the monster or the murderer. He asks the figure, "How may I help you?" Then he listens for an answer.

The next phase is the gift exchange, wherein he insists upon receiving a gift from the nightmare figure and in return gives the figure a gift. It is during this phase that the figure often changes its behavior or its presence. Nightmares, as we see them, are symbolic of inner distress or inner conflict, which, of course, can come about either through inner or outer distress and conflict. It is the gift exchange that brings about inner harmony for the child: Rarely do individuals exchange gifts with the enemy. Next, the child can draw or paint or sculpt his gifts as a reminder of befriending his dream enemy.

Harry

To demonstrate our photo art therapy method of working with dreams, Harry agreed to work on a dream which he had dreamt the night before he met with Corbit for a therapy session. Harry is a 46-year-old man who had taken part in an extensive photo art therapy program, in addition to this dream therapy. The reader may want to consult Chapters 3, 8, and 9 for other examples of Harry's photo artwork.

Harry: Well, what happened is this morning I woke up about five, which is not unusual. I usually wake up early in the morning. I went in to make a cup of coffee and I saw a piece of scrap paper on the floor. I reached down to pick it up and as I bent down I couldn't straighten up again and I got this excruciating pain in my lower back. It went sideways from one side to the other, and I couldn't straighten back up. So I stood there for quite some time, I think it was probably about ten minutes, and thought about waking up my wife to come and help me. What I really wanted to do was to lie on the floor, but I couldn't even straighten up enough to do that.

So you couldn't even lie on the floor?

Harry: No. I couldn't do anything except stand there bent over. So what I did is that I gradually managed to straighten up. And the pain subsided slightly. And then I walked around a little bit, or limped around, basically. I felt like an old man, holding my back and trying to stand up. Then I went out for the newspaper and I had to pick it up with my toes because I couldn't bend over. I wanted to read the paper but I couldn't find a place where I could sit down and be comfortable. I finally sat in a hard back chair at the table, a dining room chair.

Had you had any problems with your back before?

Harry: No. The only time I've had back problems was—what was it? Over twenty years ago I fell one time, but I didn't break anything. It was a sprain. But this doesn't seem to be related to that. It doesn't feel like the same thing.

And where is the pain?

Harry: It's right across my lower back. It feels like it goes across sideways. But, anyway, where was I? I got the paper and I sat down and if I sat up really straight and didn't move, then I could read the paper. So I did that, then I would get up and walk around once in a while. Finally it got a little looser and it wasn't quite so painful, it was just aggravating. Then I went to work about eight o'clock, and it wasn't too bad.

And then I came up here. In the car, I was relating it to a dream I had last night. The dream I had was that I had to go somewhere. I don't know where. And it seemed that it was a long way away, about 20 miles or so. It was a long way away, and I went by myself, and I had to go bring something back. And all the way I was walking through really sticky mud. I could hardly lift my feet. It was like trying to walk through gumbo—gumbo mud. So I walked all the way

up there, and whatever it was I was getting I carried back. On the way back there was somebody with me, and I don't know who it was.
Was it male or female?
Harry: Male, I think. I really couldn't tell you. And it wasn't anybody specific. I was walking back, and I walked through mud and I remember thinking in my dream that if I could just walk through shallow water, not even shoe height, but shallow water an inch deep or so that it would be a lot easier walking. So I would try to find easier places to walk, but most of the time it was really hard.
Would it relieve your back if you were going through the easier parts?
Harry: At that time in my dream my back didn't hurt. It was just that my feet were really heavy and I couldn't lift my feet. So I was walking along, and then I moved from mud into some kind of a barn yard and there was a lot of chicken shit everywhere.
A lot of chickens?
Harry: I didn't see any chickens, but there was chicken shit everywhere. I didn't see any chickens. And the only animals I saw were two lambs that somebody was herding through a gate or a corral or some kind of an enclosure. I went in that direction toward them, and I was still walking through mud, and not only mud, but chicken shit at the same time. And everything was sort of covered with white, seemed like it was chicken manure. It was on top of my head, but I think I had on a cap of some sort. And whoever was herding these two animals was just covered with chicken shit and then I was kind of slogging through that and the mud and everything and that was the last I remember. I awakened about five. It was pouring down rain, by the way. It was really raining hard. And I got up and then I went to the kitchen, and, as I was saying, I had this back problem. First of all, I don't have back problems, and, secondly, I rarely have bad dreams. I usually have very pleasant dreams.
So this was an unusual circumstance.
Harry: Yes, it really was unusual.

(At this point, as Harry posed for a photograph of himself in the dream, he again experiences severe pain in his back. He began the artwork on his dream poster, and as he worked on the poster, he continued talking.)

Harry: So then I came up here and I was telling you about it, and I got into this pose for this photograph showing how in the dream I was carrying something, and it seemed like it was a real rough square board — it was square, it wasn't a board shape, two inches or four inches square.
And long? How long was it?
Harry: It was five or six feet long.
That's pretty long.
Harry: It was good and hefty. It didn't seem so heavy, but it was rough textured. It was rough textured like it was an unfinished piece of lumber. At first I thought I was carrying a cross, but then it didn't seem like a cross. It seemed like this straight plank of some sort. While I was getting into a pose to

Figure 6-1. Harry's Dream

take a photograph to show what it was like carrying that, all of a sudden I had that same pain across my back. So I got into the right pose, whatever it was. And I suspect that last night that I was in that posture while I was sleeping and must have strained those muscles. Anyway I have this picture here and just looking at it right now, it looks heavy.

It does.

Harry: It looks like a burden of some sort.

What kind of wood do you think it was?

Harry: It was rough wood.

Like a pine? Because you said it's not too heavy.

Harry: It didn't feel heavy, but the main thing that I can remember is that I could feel the texture in my right hand. I don't remember feeling it in my left hand, but I could feel it in my right hand. That it was rough textured, unfinished . . .

And you're right handed, aren't you?

Harry: Yes. It was a rough textured, unfinished board of some sort. And right now I have no idea of what that might be symbolic of, but it's something obviously, some burden that I'm trying to carry around through the shit.

And the chickens must have been roosting pretty high to hit this other man on the head and everything.

Harry: I guess. It seemed to be everywhere. The association I can make right now is that when I was growing up on a farm, my job was to clean the chicken house, and I hated it. What we would have to do, my brother and I, we would have to take a hoe and scrape all the chicken manure out. We did that, I don't know how often, once a month probably.

Probably once a week.

Harry: No. I don't think that often, because it would build up and we would have to scrape it out, and I didn't like that job one bit.

Because my mother used to raise chickens. I didn't have to clean the chicken house, my brother did. But I recall every weekend, he was out there cleaning it.

Harry: Once a week?

Umhumm. He was cleaning it every weekend.

Harry: I really don't remember, but I know it was the worst job on the farm.

Umhumm.

Harry: It seemed to me like I had to do it, and it seemed to me my brother helped me, but I can't really remember.

Maybe you traded off. Maybe you did it every other weekend.

Harry: That's possible. I really don't know. So there's that association from the past. And as far as what's going on presently, there's a lot of things going on at work. We had a cutback at work and we have to . . . But it doesn't seem any different from the usual. We usually have financial problems at work.

But, what do you think of when you think of chicken shit?

Harry: Well, paperwork, that's one thing.

Nuisance things.

Harry: Yes. Nuisance things. Paperwork. I hate paperwork. I really can't exaggerate how much I hate paperwork.

And, chicken shit things are like things that really aren't necessary, I would say, because they are organizational things, or things that somebody that wants a lot of structure in an organization wants to keep track of you and keep track of the things that you do.

Harry: Yes. But actually I'm not having any problems at work, any more than usual . . . usually I don't have too many problems. I have taken on this new administrative job, but it's not very much of a job. (Harry points to his artwork.) I'm making this plank here and it's too big.

What is a cross without the cross?

Harry: I don't know. It's a straight line.

What could you do with something like that? With a plank like that? It looks like you could use it for building a fence or a gate post or something like that.

Harry: Yes. In my dream it didn't seem like it was to build anything. It seemed just like a burden.

A burden?

Harry: Or, it wasn't anything useful.

So you're going through this . . .

Harry: But whatever it was, it was unformed . . . and that seems to be important that it was not finished. It was . . .

The board wasn't finished.

Harry: Yes. It was rough . . . is that glue?

Umhumm.

Harry: I'll start with this here. Maybe I'll pull this background off and use it for . . . for the other person.

Good idea.

Harry: My back still hurts. I stirred it up again just now when I posed for this picture.

But, in the photograph your body pose doesn't look like it's contorted in any way.

Harry: It does to me.

Does it?

Harry: Yes.

You've got your legs moving forward. Did you feel that you were slumped over somewhat holding that?

Harry: Just like this. And then whoever was with me was sort of to the right. I'll put this background here. And then, the scene I'm going to make is with the two lambs. They were small.

When you mention lambs, what do you think about?

Harry: Religion is one thing. The farm. Living on a farm.

When I think of lambs, I think of lambs going to slaughter.

Harry: I don't. This was a barnyard of some sort.

Were they young, very young lambs?

Harry: Yes. They were young, not too old. It doesn't seem to me like they were the most important things, but that was part of it. The most important thing was wading through all that mud. I'm going to make a bunch of footprints. I'm going to . . . trying to walk through the mud. I'll just put a whole bunch of these. These footprints represent about twenty miles of muddy road.

Where did you get the twenty miles?

Harry: I don't know. But it seems like it was about twenty miles. It was a long way.

That's quite a distance! Did you walk the whole thing in your dream?

Harry: Yes. Well, no, I didn't. I walked part of the way there, and then picked it up near the end of the journey coming back.

But you knew you walked a long distance. Your person that accompanied you on the way back, did he ever offer to carry your burden for you.

Harry: No. And I just now noticed that he wasn't carrying anything with me.

'Cause that's a long way to carry that burden. I wonder how far Christ carried his cross?

Harry: Twelve stations. Twelve stations, however far that was. How far was it?

I don't know.

Harry: I don't either. I don't know how to do those . . .

The symbolism of the lambs and the burden, carrying that wooden plank . . .

Harry: Will you take another picture . . . the person herding the lambs? . . . (After the photograph is taken) . . . I'm having a little trouble with this, because in the dream it was from the perspective of myself carrying the plank. Looking at it this way when I'm drawing it, I'm doing this artwork from another perspective. I'm thinking what it would look like from the other side, I probably should have done it from the other point of view.

Going the opposite direction?

Harry: No. From the point of view of looking at it this way.

Coming forward towards you? In the poster, you would be coming forward?

Harry: In the picture, it would be whatever this person would be seeing from this way. But that's alright, I'm just doing it for now from this point of view. So, this sheepherder is about here, and the lambs are coming through some kind of a gate here. Let's see if I can do that. Yes. That's about the way it was, like the entrance was off to the right. And these two animals were . . . sheep. I had a coat on, by the way. Maybe I'll make a coat out of something. I suppose that these other people in the dream were just parts of me that . . . the shepherd was a part of me. He wasn't carrying any burden.

But he had a lot of responsibility, having to take care of those sheep.

Harry: Yeah. It didn't seem like it was a big deal but . . .

And the other part of you, that figure that came with you on the way back, he wasn't much help.

Harry: No. He wasn't any help at all. It didn't seem like . . . I don't think that figure is important; I don't know exactly what that might represent. Whatever this dream was, it sure gave me a pain in the back. I keep cutting off the top of my head. I did it in both of these. Now this person had chicken manure all over him. Is this (white crayon) going to show up?

It won't show up too much. Would you like to use blue or gray? Gray would be good.

Harry: This sheepherder here, and particularly on his head . . .

That's a lot of chicken shit.

Harry: I'm showing it as gray, but it was white in this area. And I think he had a cap on, in fact, I think I had a cap on. Some kind of a cap. I can't draw sheep. You got a sheep around here somewhere?

I might have a book with some.

Harry: You've got this one (picking up a folk art lamb).

I've got lots of wolves (pointing out some wolves in the book).

Harry: Except this is a full grown one. I'll just fake it. And they were sort of, not going in different directions, but kind of separating.

You don't think that the plank that you were carrying had anything to do with building fences or gates or anything like that?

Harry: It didn't seem like it. It doesn't seem like it had anything to do with anything, except it was, like I said, it was rough. Oh! You know what I realized, I've got my wrong hand. I was feeling it with my right hand, and I could feel the texture, not splinters, but just unfinished.

Rough.

Harry: It was r-o-u-g-h. There was a building of some sort over here, too. I might as well stick with brown; it seemed to be brown. This was like a barn, but there wasn't any. . . . I remember clearly that there was an opening here, and I was going in that direction through that opening. And what was off through that opening, I couldn't tell you, I have no idea.

The lambs are going the opposite way, they're coming out.

Harry: That's right. They were going in the opposite direction, they were coming out. They were coming this way.

Toward you?

Harry: No, not toward me, but off to . . . like I drew it here. And I was going to go through this opening and on beyond there someplace. And this person herding the sheep seemed to be fairly irrelevant. Just happened to be there. He wasn't particularly blocking my way or anything, but just happened to be there at that particular junction.

What do you think of that person? Was he smart? Or was he . . .

Harry: He was covered in shit . . . that's what he was, in the chicken manure. This needs to be black, or dark, dark brown. It was all mud.

Where did the chicken shit start?

Harry: About where I drew these people.

So, it's closer to the farmhouse? But there were no chickens?

Harry: No. I didn't see chickens. And all this was just covered with chicken manure, white chicken manure. This entire area here, beginning about here. So it was like I had to walk through all this mud, sticky mud that was sticking to the bottom of my feet, and trying to wade through there.

Was it smelly, too? Did you smell anything?

Harry: No. I didn't smell anything, but then I had to walk through chicken shit, too, and get it all over me and everything. It wasn't very pleasant, in fact, it was really an unpleasant dream. Well, this is good (talking about an oil stick he was using), just smear this all over you. It was just everywhere.

Like he's almost submerged in chicken manure.

Harry: Yes. It was like it was piled up on his head and it was on my head, too.

How about your friend, your companion? Did he have any?

Harry: I don't know. He was a real shadowy figure.

What was in the barn? Were the chickens in the barn, do you think?

Harry: It was like a farmyard, a barn or a shed or something like that. It wasn't like a house. The only thing that I remember from the first part of the dream is walking through mud. There weren't any details to it. I think that at this junction is when I woke up, at this scene that I reproduced. It seemed like a lot of trouble, wading through the mud, and . . . The way I've shown these footprints coming down through the mud here, that each one was just very difficult. I'd have to pull my feet out. My feet would stick in the mud and I kept trying to find an easier path.

That would give you a backache, if you walked for 40 miles, 20 miles each way.

Harry: It was real hard, it was difficult walking.

I would think it would be difficult on the back, thinking of pulling each foot out, thinking of the strain in the lower back muscles there.

Harry: Yes, it was a strain. It was very much of a chore, and for no obvious purpose. It was just hard work with no gain. But I was going someplace, I wasn't just walking. I had a goal.

Did you own the farm here? Was that your farm?

Harry: I don't know. It seems like it was somehow related to the farm where I grew up. But in my dream it wasn't like "this is my farm"; it was more like "this is just a barnyard of some sort with these two animals."

Were there lambs on the farm where you grew up?

Harry: Yes.

Can you associate anything at all in what's happening in your life right now to what was going on then, anything on a feeling level? feeling under pressure? feeling separated from people? feeling neglected? whatever?

Harry: Not anything specific. One of the things that occurred to me is I've been reading a book about India. It doesn't have anything to do with farming. The book is a book of short stories, and the stories are really universal stories. Most of the stories have to do with sexual encounters of some kind. I don't know if that's relevant or not, but I've been reading those. And I was reading them before I went to bed last night; I was reading a couple of the stories. That's possibly valid, but none of them were about farmyards. They were tragedies, people in some kind of tragic lives. As far as my own farm childhood, that wasn't very pleasant.

You did have to work on the farm, you had to clean out the chicken house. Probably do some other farm chores.

Harry: Yes. Probably no more than other farm kids. I mean, I don't feel like I was singled out. I didn't like it much. I mean they don't call it chores for nothing. They really are chores.

When you were a kid did you think of when you grew up you'd never be a farmer?

Harry: I don't know if I did when I was a kid, but when I was a little older I for sure thought that I'd get an education so that I'd never be a farmer. I wouldn't mind living on a farm, but I'm not going to work on a farm. If I ever go back to a farm, it would be hiring somebody to do all the work.

There's a lot of burden there in carrying that plank. If it was 20 miles each way, then it was 40 miles.

Harry: It was a long way.

That's a long distance to carry that plank.

Harry: I wasn't carrying it on the way up, just on the way back.

Just on the way back?

Harry: So I went to get it. Apparently I was going to get whatever it is I was carrying.

You know even twenty miles carrying a plank is a long way. That's a beast of burden in a way, isn't it?

Harry: Yea. But it wasn't like it was a burden, it was like it was something that I went to get on purpose and was bringing back for a purpose. It wasn't like something I was just carrying around for no good reason. And I have no idea right now what it is or what it might represent, but it was some goal-oriented task that I assigned myself. It doesn't seem like somebody told me to do it, it seems like something that I had taken on for myself.

And it was rough so it wasn't finished. It wasn't something that you were ready to put into a piece of furniture or anything like that.

Harry: No. I wasn't going to do that at least for a while. And I don't know where I was going. This farm was not the final destination. I was going through there to somewhere else.

It wouldn't be firewood, would it, or something like that?

Harry: No. It was a board; it wasn't a log.

Something had been done to it.

Harry: Yes. It was a rough finished board of some sort. So I don't know, I just know that I had gone to get it and I was going somewhere with it. And I was going through this piece of a dream to get there. This was a very unpleasant, difficult part, and I don't know where the final goal was. It was like I was in the middle of it.

Just to give you a little relief from this pressure, it might be a good idea if, in your imagination, you set the board down or find a place where you can set it down so that you don't have to keep carrying it and putting all that strain on your back.

Harry: Yes. I might get this other guy to carry it for me.

That's a good idea.

Harry: It doesn't seem right to put it down. That doesn't feel right. It feels more like I'm a little helpless carrying it.

So if you had something or somebody else, a cart or a person that would help to carry it might relieve some of that pressure. It's too much on yourself, too much of a burden for you to carry by yourself.

Harry: Yes. It's not just what I was carrying, but the terrain while I was trying to walk. The mud was difficult. And I don't think that I mentioned since you turned the tape recorder on that it seemed that there were some areas that I could walk easier if there was some water. If I could find a path, not a path, but if I could find some areas where there was a little bit of water that was maybe a half inch or an inch deep, it wasn't so hard walking. It wasn't some sticky mud and it was easier going. It would sometimes make it a little easier that way. And I seem to have this vague memory that whoever this other person is with me, I would mention that to him, that we could find an easier path.

But he still didn't offer to help you?

Harry: No. He's a very quiet person. I suppose this is some part of myself that's a silent companion of some sort.

Well, having two of something could indicate that this is fairly close to consciousness. So, you have the two figures here (pointing to the poster), and the two here. It might be something within your grasp.

Harry: That's interesting. Why do you suppose these are young animals rather than mature animals?

Maybe it's something new in your life.

Harry: They were lambs. Obviously they were lambs.

They're not threatening. I don't think that lambs were threatening.

Harry: They weren't threatening.

Usually people think of lambs as sweet.

Harry: They were white lambs, I know that. White lambs and white chicken shit.

Purity? Or purity of thought?

Harry: Or just that most lambs are white. When I was a kid I had sheep and I raised lambs.

Did you like them? Did you enjoy the little lambs?

Harry: The little lambs, I did, not the sheep so much. The lambs were fun to have around.

You'd think this would have been sheep shit, wouldn't you?

Harry: No. It was chicken.

I know. But, with the lambs around you'd think it would have been sheep rather than chicken. Chicken shit just gives me that idea . . .

Harry: Not too important.

It's really just a total nuisance. Well, how about taking this home with you and putting it somewhere where you can look at it, and not try to work on it too hard, but just when you see it allow your mind to come up with some new associations to it. And maybe we can get some new material on Tuesday from it.

Harry: O.K. I can do that.

Another thing we could do is to do some active imagination with it to carry the dream on and see what happens with that. Why don't we do that on Tuesday.

Harry: O.K. I hope I don't forget this. It's real vivid right now.

You won't forget it. You've got it all down here and the rest of it is on the tape.

Harry: I was trying to think if there was any more to it, any more images. It was mostly white. There was no color whatsoever.

You said you had a jacket and he had a jacket. What color were they?

Harry: Black. Yeah. I'll draw them.

So it was mostly black and white and some brown.

Harry: Yeah. There wasn't any color. Maybe I'll cut out a jacket. It wasn't a colorful image at all. It was just drab. I'm going to cut out . . . I'll do that.

Okay.

Harry: It was really basic.

Was that a drab life you lived when you lived on the farm? Was there any excitement?

Harry: That's a good question. The best thing about it was all the young animals, the baby animals. The pigs and the goats . . . not goats, sheep.

How old were you at that time?

Harry: I lived there from about five until the eighth grade.

So it was during the time that you could associate being around the age of your son, possibly?

Harry: Yes. Same age. We moved from the farm when I was just starting the eighth grade. Actually it wasn't a very long period of time. It was about eight years.

Just as a guess I'd wonder if your life isn't seeming bogged down and lackluster, that it would be great if there were a little more excitement in your life?

Harry: That's a possibility.

Having to go through a lot of repetitious things that are required of you? Things that aren't fun? No new adventure?

Harry: That's not really true though. I had a really interesting summer.

But that's over.

Harry: Yes. It's over now, but it's starting back into the regular working year again.

Into the chicken shit?

Harry: It doesn't feel that I'm bogged down now in my professional life. Maybe, I think it's something much more basic than that . . . much more subtle than that. And I'm not exactly sure what it is. It probably has to do with aging, not being as energetic, maybe. I'm trying to think of what might have stirred this up. I was . . . that book that I've read might have been part of it.

And what was the title of the book?

Harry: *Afternoon at Coracini's,* or something like that. That was the title of one of the stories. It was a book of short stories written by an Indian author and almost all of the stories are set in India. One was set in Great Britain . . . fascinating stories. They're really wild. That's part of it. And I've started this group with Kay, but that's not a burden. It doesn't seem like a burden, it feels like something more interesting.

This pole that you have is a giant phallic shape, too.

Harry: Well, I don't know about that, but it was heavy. It wasn't so much heavy, it just was there. It was a pretty good size.

There aren't many soft feminine curves here, in your entire picture. You have lots of poles, lots of straight lines. Your house is all straight lines. The lambs are the most feminine, the softest.

Harry: Nothing felt very feminine about it. Mostly it was really unpleasant. It wasn't a nightmare, I mean, it wasn't anything fearful. I wasn't afraid. It was just trudging along trying to get my feet out of the mud. It was tiring.

I think the most interesting part to me is that your body picked up the message and is really giving you the message to pay attention. Whatever it is that's going on with you, pay attention.

Harry: I wish I had a little better grasp of what it is I'm supposed to pay attention to.

Because it comes from the unconscious, it's all in the dark.

Harry: Maybe I don't have to know what it is, I just need to do it.

Well, sometimes it just takes a while for it to seep up through.

Harry: I have the feeling that it doesn't matter too much whether I know what it is as long as I pay attention to it.

And have somebody to help you. I think that's one of the big messages from this is that it's important that you ask for help and not try to carry it all yourself. Because if the burden is shifted somewhat, I don't know that your back will bother you so much.

Harry: I'm not so much interested in help as I am in getting through it. I'd like to know what's beyond here and get through whatever this is that I've been trying to get through. Get on with whatever is beyond that. Maybe what I ought to do is to try to figure out what's on the other side.

If you want to on Tuesday, we'll do some active imagination and continue the dream on.

Harry: O.K. That might be useful.

Well, let's quit for today.

Harry's dream was very powerful, powerful enough to cause him severe back pain. He had first experienced the back pain when he picked up a piece of paper, then the morning newspaper, then again when he assumed the dream pose where he was carrying the plank. Although there were many implications as to what the dream might mean to Harry, there was no ah-ha! for him, no sudden insight as to its meaning. Harry speculated that it might have something to do with an exotic book of short stories that he had been reading. He had, in fact, been reading a story from the book the evening before the dream. He also thought that the dream, possibly because of his back pain, might have something to do with aging and, more likely, the debilitating circumstances which come with aging.

Harry rejected any suggestion that the dream symbols of the lambs or carrying the plank might indicate Christian or sacrificial themes. He also rejected the thought that being bogged down in the mud had anything to do with his current life. On the other hand, Harry was able to associate symbols in his dream to early childhood memories of living on a farm. He found life to be uncomplicated at that time, and associated pleasant memories to his interactions with the baby animals.

Sometimes a dream such as this requires only time and patience for its meaning to become apparent. On the other hand, because the dream was so vivid, Harry was eager to decipher the dream, and we decided that it might be useful for us to continue the dream in active imagination.

Active Imagination

Jung's theory of active imagination originally came out of his studies of the ancient art of alchemy—the transforming of base materials into gold (Collected Works, Vol. 14). The alchemists, he discovered, were actually philosophers searching for the "true" gold—the gold of the soul—and their projections were built upon the *prima materia*, or base material, reflecting the inner workings of their own psyches. Jung said that the secret of alchemy was the transcendent function, the transformation of personality through the blending and fusion of the noble with the base components, of the differentiated with the inferior functions, of the conscious with the unconscious (Collected Works, Vol. 7).

Jung's concept of the transcendent function was one of his important contributions to the field of psychology. He saw the importance of facilitating communication between the conscious and the unconscious aspects of the personality to bring about a new and more healthy attitude. The unconscious was not, in his opinion, to be condemned, but to be recognized for its significance in its role of compensating one's conscious position (Collected Works, Vol. 8). This, he felt, could be accomplished through the transcendent function, or in the integration of unconscious material into consciousness. Active imagination was the technique that he used to perform this transition.

The active imagination method permits a confrontation between the conscious and the unconscious from an ego standpoint, thereby producing a third or centering point in the psyche. Through this process when a figure or image containing elements of the opposites appears, as in a dream or a fantasy, this figure or image becomes a symbol uniting the opposites and facilitating a transition from one attitude to another.

Active imagination is a psychic state wherein the formless archetypes in the unconscious acquire manifest forms which become active and autonomous. The active imagination images take on a life of their own, and symbolic events develop according to their own logic, if conscious reason does not interfere. Active imagination is, Jung (Collected Works, Vol 9, Pt. 1, p. 190) says, "part dream, part vision, or dream mixed with vision." It is a method to observe one's stream of interior images. Jung would have his clients focus their attention upon some aspect of their dream which was memorable, yet unintelligible, or upon a spontaneous vision. They were to continue their concentration, at the same time observing any changes taking place in the dream-images or visions. They were not to make judgment of their active imagination, but simply to note the process objectively.

According to Jung (Collected Works, Vol. 18), to engage in active imagination one must begin by concentrating on a mental picture, then when it begins to stir, "the image becomes enriched by details, it moves and develops... And so when we concentrate on an inner picture and when we are careful not to interrupt the natural flow of events, our unconscious will produce a series of images which make a complete story" (p. 172).

Another important feature of active imagination is that by getting in touch with symbols from the unconscious through this process, one can not only find direction, but can access new sources of energy (Adler, 1948). "These symbols have the capacity of controlling undifferentiated and primitive libido," according to Adler (p. 64). Jung felt the symbol to be a transformer of energy: unassimilated energy which is locked into the unconscious in the form of neurotic symptoms can be transformed into energy and integrated into the conscious attitude through the use of the symbol. This ego assimilation process can take place through a dream or other means of unconscious expression, such as active imagination.

As an example, a woman who was a student of Jungian psychology shared the following brief cryptic dream: A brown horse was standing in front of a white horse; both were immobilized. When she took the dream into active imagination, she led the white horse around and in front of the brown horse. Immediately, the white horse raced off across a stream, and the brown horse followed. Along with this imagery, she experienced a new flow of energy and enthusiasm.

Harry and I had agreed to continue his working with his dream using Jung's method of active imagination. We recorded the session.

I'd like you to get as relaxed as possible and go back into your dream state as far as you can go. It's best to close your eyes, and first go through your body in your imagination to let go of tension. Any tension that you find in any part of your body, just let that go. Tell yourself relax, relax. Relax all of the muscles in your body. Feel yourself letting go and getting more and more relaxed. Now, try to find yourself at the beginning of your dream. Tell the dream as it's happening.

Harry: OK. I'm walking along sort of like a stream bed of real shallow water. Not all of it is shallow water, some of it is mud, and it's a little sticky, the clinging kind of mud. And it's sticking to my feet. It's hard to move. It seems like I'm going upstream or north and I'm on a kind of mission to get something. I'm by myself, and it's very difficult going. It's hard to walk.

I try to pick out easier places to walk and easier places where it isn't so sticky. I walk along and then I'm coming back south or back down stream again. And I've gotten whatever it is that I went to get. There's a companion with me and he's to my right. I can't really see him very clearly, he's to my right a little bit behind me. And it's still very sticky, muddy going and again I try to find the easiest place to walk. This water is shallow water not even as high as my shoes, an inch deep or half inch deep. And it always seems like it is easier when I can find those places. And then all of a sudden I realize that I'm carrying this . . . it's some kind of a board or something. I'm carrying it on my right shoulder and I can feel the texture of the board on my hands, in my right hand. I think I'm carrying the end of it in my left hand, and holding it steady with my right hand, then carrying it on my right shoulder. It's a rough feeling plank or board of some sort that seems to be about four or five feet long and it's maybe two or three inches on the side square. And I can feel the texture of it. It's not splintery, but it's rough, like it has a little sand in it.

About that time as I'm walking along I notice that I'm coming near a barnyard, it seems like a barnyard. There's a building off ahead of me and to the left of some kind of barn and there are animals around there. There's a fence between me and the barn. Then there's an opening in the fence ahead of me and a little bit to the right. There's a man coming through the opening in the fence more or less toward me, but he was a little off to the right. And there seem to be young lambs and they were kind of jerking around and being playful. They were sort of separating and it seems like they're going in opposite directions, in not quite parallel directions.

Another thing that I notice is that there's white chicken shit all over everything, all over the man and all over me. It seems like I have a cap on or he has a cap on or both of us do. It's just completely white, covered with chicken shit. It's all over everything. It's real white, like snow. It's all over the floor, I mean the ground. It's all over the barnyard. It's all over the fence. It's all over everything. And that's about it. I seem to be at this point just kind of walking toward the fence.

What I'd like you to do now is stay with the dream, but continue the dream. To continue it, you can interact with these dream figures, or you can do whatever you want to. You can bring some closure to your dream or some insight to the dream.

Harry: Another thing that I forgot to mention is that I have a kind of dark coat on. It seems black or dark, a jacket of some sort. Well I guess I'll keep walking. And the other guy, whoever it is, my companion just kind of walks along with me and the other, the shepherd continues coming along herding the sheep. He doesn't seem to pay any attention. Let's see . . . I've got this board and what am I going to do with it? It seems like I'd better keep carrying it. So, I'm going to go between the shepherd and the sheep, so I'm cutting off a lot . . . But still he doesn't seem to pay any attention, doesn't seem to be interested. Let's see . . . so I'll just go ahead in front of him and walk on through, still carrying the board. I don't see the barnyard at all on the other side. I don't think there's a fence on the other side, so I'll just walk on through. So, I'm coming out of the barnyard, and I'm also coming out of the chicken shit. Let's see, it's more yellow grassland, or maybe a pasture or something. It's a lot more pleasant than the mud. Easy walking.

I'll keep walking, keep going. I guess the guy is still with me, my companion. He doesn't seem to be any help, he's just with me. We're walking along, and I guess there's a stream here. It must be on the right. And parallel with the stream is a pasture with the grass. It sure is a relief to be out of the mud with the chicken shit and to be on solid ground. I'm going along and I'm carrying this board . . . and I know what I'll do, I'll build a bridge with this board that I'm carrying, so that I can get on the other side of the stream. So I'll just lay it down there, then I can walk across to the right side of it.

I wonder what my companion is going to do because there's not room for the two of us on this board, on this plank. So I guess I'll walk across the plank and get to the right side of the stream, and he's still with me. I guess he just sort of floated across. He doesn't seem to need anything to walk on. I can leave this plank, I don't have to carry it any longer. We can continue on along this stream, but now I'm on the other side. Keep walking down the stream. Now I can walk a little more jauntily because I don't have to carry anything. Maybe I'll start whistling or something like that or singing. It feels pretty good to hike along the stream bed without having to carry anything.

My companion there seems to be a spirit, he's kind of floating along. He's kind of a shadow, sticking with me. He's not a dark figure; it's somehow more spiritual. I don't know where I'm going. Downstream, I guess. Oh, it seems I'm back where I started at the beginning of the dream that I was going in the opposite direction. Now I'm going back to where I started, except now it's real easy going. I'm kind of stuck here, I go back wherever I started. There doesn't seem to be anybody around. I'm not sure where to go from here.

So, anyway, I'm back where I started, it's an open area. Pleasant. I don't know if it's a field . . . it's an outdoors area of some sort. A pasture. No place to sit down, no logs. Completely open. I wish I had a place to sit down, but I'll just stand. I have this urge to start the whole thing over again. Something purposeful. I'd just as soon not have to wade through all the chicken shit again. My companion is always about three feet away and off to the right. He doesn't ever say anything. He just sort of knows. Wherever it is, it's back where I started.

It was a clockwise trip. The chicken shit was on the other side. I wonder what would happen if I went downstream instead of upstream? Maybe this is like past and future, going upstream is like going back to the past and downstream the future? I don't really want to. I had the feel that this dream was like going backwards.

I'm getting away from the active imagination; I'm starting to come out of it. Actually, I'd like to go downstream. No, I don't want to. I'll wait until another time. I'll be ready to stay there and wait. I think in my next trip, I'll go downstream.

Is that the opposite direction from where the sheep and the herder are?

Harry: Yes. And it's on the other side of the river, too, or stream or whatever it is. It's small, like a stream.

What does the water look like?

Harry: It's clear. I'll tell you what it is, it's the stream from when I was a child on the farm. There was a stream running on the property.

Did you walk across it a lot of times in your childhood?

Harry: I had to go across it to get to school.

Did you have a bridge?

Harry: No, I just jumped across it. It was small.

Was there any chicken shit around?

Harry: Oh, yes. At the house where the barnyard was. I'm associating that our house and the barn were on one side of the stream and the school was on the other. So I had to go across to go to school on the other side. It was about a mile. It sort of feels like going back and picking up some pieces of childhood. I guess we could always make a case for upstream being in the past, and downstream being towards the future.

What about the sheep herder?

Harry: Beats me. I don't know. I was going in the opposite direction. I think there are probably some other animals in the barn, cows, not particularly important. I know there are some other animals. Cows. I don't want to go too much further . . . going back to childhood.

Maybe once you looked around and gained a different perspective, you wouldn't have to go through it again.

Harry: It might be no more complicated than that, I'm still carrying some of that burden.

It seems to me, too, when you mentioned the lambs spreading out, that they might be difficult to herd if they're going in two different directions.

Harry: Could be my brother and sister, going in different directions. Well, I guess the only reasonable way to look at this is that they're parts of myself. This part carrying the planks was a self part, the more simple part. And I don't know what the other part was, it would be useful to figure out.

Neither of the other two parts were verbal.

Harry: No they didn't say anything.

That one is a laborer; this one is a laborer, too (pointing to the figures on the poster). He's the sheep herder, but as you talked about him he didn't seem to be very bright. He wouldn't even look at you. He seemed oblivious to you. And just allowing himself to be covered with the shit, he didn't brush it off or anything. He just walked with it.

Harry: Yes. So did I. I know one thing you'd never get me back on a farm. Not as the farmer. I might live there and get somebody else to do all the work. I never knew anyone who lived on a farm who wanted to go back.

A lot of work.

Harry: I'll tell you what, it's a burden. It's not so much the work, but it's that you always have to be there. You have to milk the cows everyday, twice a day whether you like it or not.

And you've got to feed the chickens.

Harry: You've got to feed the chickens. It's not the amount of work, but it's a real burden.

Did you have to clean up after the chickens?

Harry: Oh, yes, sure. It's a constant thing that you just can't . . . if you wanted to go off on vacation, you'd have to make arrangements with someone to take care of things. You just can't get up and leave, there's no freedom. Unless you had a manager, that would be different. I wouldn't mind doing it if I had a manager, because I like to be outdoors. And I like having animals around.

It is strange to think about that time. We lived on that farm when I was in the first grade . . . well, actually it must have been before then; it must have been from when I was about four and a half or five, until the beginning of the eighth grade. That's not very long when you think about it, seven years.

Well it depends on how you look at it.

Harry: It's long in a child's life, but in an adult's life, it's not so long. Seven years, that's not very long. But when I think about my childhood, it seems like that was all of it.

Well it was almost. Those were the most indelible years, probably. At about five is the period when you really begin noticing things around you.

Harry: But before that we lived in town, and after that we moved back to the same town. I was going into the eighth grade then. But it seems like that was an important time. Most of it was pretty chaotic.

Did your dad live on the farm with you?

Harry: Well, when he was there. He wasn't there much.

So, your mom had most of the burden?

Harry: Yes. He was never there much because he was always off to a mental hospital somewhere. Or when he was around, you know what he used to do? He would, this is a Nebraska farm, a two-story frame house and no insulation at all. It was up on the plains. Those Canadian cold fronts would come down and nothing could stop them. And it's really cold there. So he used to move into town and live in a hotel and leave the family out on the farm. He was a jerk. He was really a jerk. And when he wasn't doing that, he was in a mental hospital or off shacked up with somebody. He always had a whole bunch of women there. He'd get shacked up with somebody for a while. I've pieced that together since then, and that's what he was doing. And other people have filled me in some. He was pretty much of a selfish person. And he was very violent; I was scared. So we, the kids, anyway, I don't know about my mother, were always glad when he left. We hated it when he'd show up. He'd show up and stay for a few days or a week, sometimes longer when there were crops to be put in or harvesting of something.

Trying to straighten everybody out?

Harry: No. He didn't do that. It was like, some things he just had to be there for like if you had to plant a crop or harvest the corn or something. But when he didn't absolutely have to be there, he wasn't very much around, which was great. And when he was there, it was as if everyone was walking on eggs, because you didn't know for sure if he was going to do something crazy, blow up.

So did you stay out of his way as much as you could?

Harry: I did. My older brother caught most of the brunt of his craziness. I remember one incident when I was about, I'm guessing probably eight or nine years old. We had a lot of guns in my house on the farm, all sorts of guns, two or three shotguns. I had a shotgun and a rifle myself. I think I must have had them from the time I was about eight or nine. So I was very familiar with firearms, and I just told him one time if he ever lay a hand on me, I'd just plain kill him. And I meant it, too.

I bet you would have.

Harry: And I would have because he was very dangerous. He used to knock my brother clear across the room. He did that to me once, and I told him after that I'd just kill him if he did it again, and he never really hurt me after that. Scared the daylights out of me sometimes, but never hurt me. And he used to slap my sister around quite a bit. He really was hard on my brother. And also he would promise you things and then renege. He did that all the time. You couldn't believe him. But he was a very violent person. He used to kill animals a lot.

That must have been rough on the kids.

Harry: One time we had this, I don't remember all the details, but I think there were two pigs or one pig, I don't remember, but anyway . . . Hey! Maybe this is related to this dream, come to think of it. I remember that one time we were trying to drive these pigs from one barnyard into another through the gate, and I don't know if you know anything about pigs, but they keep turning around trying to go back as we're trying to drive them somewhere. So this one pig kept turning around and trying to come back to the gate, and my dad just picked up a pitchfork and killed him. Stabbed him several times. And then he made my brother and me carry him off and bury him. And you kept wondering, if he could do that to a pig then he could do it to me. And he could have because he just lost it; he just completely lost control. His eyes glazed over and bugged out of his head. And he obviously was out of control. I have no doubt at all that he could have lost control with a child just as easily as he could with that animal.

You'd have to really tiptoe around, wouldn't you?

Harry: Oh yes. Another time he almost beat a horse to death, just almost beat him to death. I thought he never would stop.

Was he drunk at the time?

Harry: No. But I'll tell you what he did, he took a lot of psychoactive medications. He'd be in the hospital, then he'd come back. He took Thorazine, and I don't know how many. Who knows? So I don't know what effect that might have had.

Most of those would keep him under control though, wouldn't they? Maybe it was when he was off of them that he got out of control.

Harry: I don't know. I always suspected that it was his personality. Anyway he was a really violent person. One time we set up a croquet game. We had a little cocker spaniel puppy; he was really cute. I don't know how old I was; I was probably seven. We were playing croquet, and somehow or other my father got into the game, and it was fun because it was one of the few times that he would play games. He would play board games sometimes with us kids and it would be fun, but most of the time he just wouldn't bother. So he started to play croquet with us and it was kind of fun because it was like a real family. And this little cocker spaniel would run out and grab the croquet ball in his teeth like he was chasing it. And it was really funny and all the kids were laughing and it was funny to watch him, the little cocker spaniel. So he did that to my dad's ball, and he killed him with the croquet mallet. He just lost control.

Painful.

Harry: And his eyes glazed over, you know, it was terrible to watch. He just deliberately killed that little puppy dog. That was rotten just like with the pig. You never knew when he was going to be unpredictable.

That's the same kind of experiences that a lot of ritual abuse victims go through.

Harry: Unpredictable?

Unpredictable and violent and once they get attached to a little animal then that animal is killed in front of them.

Harry: This wasn't that. It didn't have the premeditated quality to it.

No. It was more craziness and irrational.

Harry: This was just crazy. What really bothered us, all of us, we talked about it sometimes, us kids; we were convinced that he could do that to a person. Just lose control.

I bet he could.

Harry: And he was real abusive to our mother. One of the things that I remember is whenever he was around and whenever he would eat meals with us it was miserable and we hated it. One of his favorite things to do was to throw all the dishes and everything out in the yard because it didn't suit him exactly right.

You mean before the dinner was eaten?

Harry: Oh, yes. Right in the middle of the dinner he would say, this doesn't taste right, or actually he would start screaming and he would pick up a bowl of beans of whatever and just open the back door and throw the whole bowl and everything out. He did that all the time. In fact, I can't recall a single meal that was pleasant, unless there was company there. Because he always controlled himself when there were other people around. In fact, other people, my cousins for example, don't believe me when I tell them of all the craziness that went on, because they never saw it. Whenever anybody was around, he could control himself. It was like he gave himself permission to be a real terrorist in the family, but he never did outside the family or when there were witnesses around. In fact, he was well-regarded by many people. I mean, they knew when he went into psychiatric hospitals all the time, but he was generally well regarded.

Did he go on his own, or did your mom send him?

Harry: Most of the time he would go by himself, but once in a while she had to put a little pressure on him. Because he would want to do something really crazy, like pick up the whole family and move to California on a moment's notice or something.

Can you relate to the plank now?

Harry: I think it probably has to do with putting some of that burden down and not carrying it around. I don't consciously do that. I don't feel that I carry a lot of burdens from my childhood, but I know I do. It's hard not to. I shudder to think how difficult it might have been had I not stood up to him. I don't know what it would have been like.

I wonder where you got the courage?

Harry: It was desperation, there wasn't any courage to it.

But your brother never did that, did he?

Harry: No, he didn't. I don't know, I thought it was desperation. I thought he would kill me, I really did. And he might have, he might very well have.

He might have.

Harry: Or injured me. He also attempted to sexually abuse my sister. This was later after my mother died, and she protected herself. I don't know the details, but she essentially left home. She left home that same day and never came back. Went to live with an aunt and uncle.

How old was she then?

Harry: Eleven. No, no, she would have been older than that. Thirteen. I don't remember, but as near as I know from what she mentioned about it, she physically protected herself and didn't allow him. And then she left that same day. I think she called my grandparents and then left home. Then, in fact, my brother and I left, too, right after that, within a week or so. We all just left. He was a very dangerous person to live with. Nobody wanted to live with him.

Well, that's a lot of chicken shit.

Harry: Yes, it is.

Bigger shit than chicken shit, though. I think of chicken shit as being more trivial, smaller things. But when we think of the massive abuse you endured...

Harry: Yes. Sometimes it seems like a lot. Sometimes it doesn't.

Although his dream provided all of the necessary elements for Harry to understand it, his active imagination seemed to be the catalyst for helping put the dream into perspective regarding his childhood. In the active imagination process the ego and the unconscious are able to interact to create a third, or transcendent function. And so it was that in discussing his dream and the active imagination symbols, Harry began to recall childhood memories of abuse and fear at the hands of his violent, mentally-ill father. Although these memories were not totally repressed, as in some cases of severe abuse, still, they remained a burden to Harry on both a conscious and unconscious level. This somatic dream forced him to take another look at his childhood situation. Sometimes when people have a history of childhood abuse, they, in turn, become abusive adults. On the other hand, in many cases the result is the opposite: the childhood abuse creates an adult sympathetic to the needs of children, even to the extent of becoming a child advocate. Harry is gentle with children, and has spent considerable time, energy, and money to help disadvantaged children.

As far as Harry's dream is concerned, his associations to his childhood abuse seemed to be a central theme. But, we might ask, is the dream and the memories of childhood abuse it apparently represented, completely resolved? No one knows. As we mentioned earlier, dreams often come in layers, so Harry might, at a later time, begin to reconsider some of the powerful symbols that appeared in his dream. In fact, some of these dream symbols show up in a poster Harry completed regarding his bouts with periodic depression (see Chapter 9). On the other hand, Harry's recounting of his childhood abuse issues and their implications seemed to bring closure to the dream.

SECTION TWO
ALLEVIATING DISTRESS AND SYMPTOMS

When most people think of therapy, they think of alleviating symptoms of distress. Most psychotherapy, with the possible exception of long-term psychoanalysis, has as its goal the relief of symptoms. The therapist helps the client to feel less depressed, less anxious or fearful, to sleep better, to become angry less often or to express anger in more acceptable ways. In this section we address ourselves to the use of photo art therapy specifically to help people with psychological symptoms or distressing circumstances.

In Chapter 7, we discuss fears and ways of helping people counter them. Of particular interest in this chapter is work with children, using a combination of photo art therapy and the sandplay method pioneered by Dora Kalff.

Chapter 8 is a discussion of intrapsychic conflicts. In addition to the ideas of C. G. Jung, we also bring in the more modern concepts of Neal Miller and John Dollard.

Chapter 9 is an attempt at analyzing photo art therapy in the treatment of apathy and depression, combining the theoretical stance of Jung and the cognitive therapy approach developed by Aaron Beck.

Chapter 10 is a case study of a woman who had an abused childhood. We show how many of the activities described in previous chapters can be combined in a short-term therapy program.

As in the first section of the book, we provide examples of art work by clients and their comments about the work.

Chapter 7

COUNTERING FEARS

Sara

Sara's mother brought her into treatment because of her fears, her lack of assertiveness, and for her practice of accepting the blame for others. Her presenting problem was the undue amount of stress she was experiencing because of some teasing from a new boy in her class.

Sara proved to be an intelligent seven-year-old girl who communicates easily. Her parents have an intact marriage. Her mother is a career woman, interested in Sara's psychological development. Sara has a younger sister who aids in creating issues of sibling rivalry.

When I (Corbit) asked Sara to name her greatest fear, she said it was Freddy Krueger. She and her mother both talked of Sara's many nightmares over the past four years. The nightmares began when Sara, at the age of three, had viewed a videotape of *Nightmare on Elm Street* brought into her home by a babysitter. Freddy Krueger, the fearsome figure in the movie, continued to haunt her through her nightmares.

After Sara's mother went to the waiting room, I asked Sara if she would be willing to draw a picture of Freddy Krueger for me. Sara drew back and voiced a definite, "No!"

I said, "We'll make him look silly. Come on, I'll help you."

Sara sat at the art table with me and watched as I began drawing the outline of Freddy Krueger.

"Now, how can we make him look silly?" I asked.

"Pour a bucket of water over his head," she suggested.

"Could you draw the bucket?" I asked.

"No," she said, reluctantly, "you do it."

I sketched the bucket over Freddy Krueger's head, and before long Sara became involved. She drew the water pouring over his head and face.

"What next?" I asked. "What else would make him look dumb?"

"Put peanut butter on him," Sara said.

I sketched a peanut butter jar while Sara colored his face and arms up to his elbows with peanut butter.

Sara soon got into the spirit of making Freddy look silly. She drew purple earrings on his ears and pimples on his face. Sara next trimmed around Freddy's figure, then cut off his shorts.

"What are you going to do with the shorts?" I asked.

"I don't know," she answered.

"How about if we put them on top of his head?" I suggested.

Sara gleefully pasted the shorts onto Freddy's head.

Next she cut out a shape from the remaining paper and pasted it where Freddy's shorts had been.

"What's that about?" I asked.

"It's his private parts," Sara giggled.

"Oh," I exclaimed, "he's got no pants on! He looks *very* silly."

The following week when Sara came in for her session she reported that she didn't have a nightmare during the entire week. We took out Freddy Krueger's portrait again and I asked whether she would be willing to do more work with it.

Sara agreed, saying that he didn't frighten her anymore.

Then I asked Sara to pose assertively with a firm stance, hands on her hips, telling Freddy Krueger to "stay out of my dreams."

It took Sara several minutes to get into her most assertive pose, but once posed, she seemed to enjoy her powerful stance. Sara repeated the phrase, "Stay out of my dreams, Freddy Krueger!" several times, each time with more enthusiasm.

We went back to the art table. Sara pasted Freddy Krueger's portrait on one half of the poster board, then trimmed her image and glued it to the other half. She took colored marking pens and drew blue lines on both sides of her image.

"That's a fence," she said, "so he can't get me."

Next, Sara added a gate. "So that I can get in and out," she said.

Sara drew green hills surrounding Freddy Krueger to keep him in.

When the poster was completed, Sara and I admired this "art masterpiece" of a powerful little girl who had changed her image of, and, in her mind, defeated the loathsome Freddy Krueger.

What creates fears in a child, or, for that matter, in an adult? Often times it is the result of a single traumatic event which later becomes a paramount memory in the child's mind, as with Sara. Additional traumas often reactivate the original fear and can generalize the feelings into different forms.

Figure 7-1. Fearless Sara and silly "Freddy Cougar."

Holly

Nine-year-old Holly, for instance, was frightened when she accidently locked herself into a school bathroom several years before coming into treatment. After her parents divorced, the fear generalized into getting onto elevators (small enclosed spaces) or to being separated from her mother. Some of Holly's fears were based on reality, such as walking to their car in the dark after an evening church service in an unsafe part of town, or the fear that something might happen to her mother when she went somewhere alone. Holly had, after all, lost her father, in essence, when her parents divorced. And who was to say that her mother, too, would not be lost to her?

Holly had worked through some original fears in her previous therapy in 1985 using photography and art. Now her father had moved from Houston to Alaska, and Holly saw him infrequently.

When Holly came back into treatment, it was because the old fears had re-emerged; fears of being away from her mother, fears of small enclosed places. Her initial separation from father had grown into a greater separation defined by distance and time.

As we talked, Holly described a trip to Alaska to visit her father where she watched part of the Ididarod sled dog race. We talked about Susan Butcher, the woman who had won the race, and the strength and endurance it takes to complete such a race.

When Holly and I discussed her pose for the photograph, she decided to become the driver of a sled dog team. This identification with Ms. Butcher, a person of skill and endurance, the simulation of a body pose, in addition to modeling power and strength, all helped the child to take on a new, more fearless, attitude. (Holly more than likely also identified with her father and his new life in Alaska.) Using the art and photography, these new feelings are then transferred into an art form and viewed as an wholistic art piece.

As we explained before, Jung identified this process of continuing a

Figure 7-2. Holly mushing her sled dogs.

dream or fantasy, and the accompanying feelings, into further imagery as "active imagination." The active imagination process is a method whereby the formless archetypes in the unconscious acquire manifest forms. These forms can take shape in paintings, clay, dance, writing, sand play, and other creative media. In active imagination images become autonomous, taking on a life of their own. One needs only to allow these images to express themselves, without judgment, to begin an active interface between conscious and unconscious. Holly began with fears of separation and loss of her parents, continued in her memory and fantasy to the image of a sled dog race, identified with the winner and her feelings of pride, strength and fearlessness. She then combined these images and feelings with her own image of herself as the driver of a dog sled, with the feelings of control and strength she had imagined in the woman who had won the race in Alaska. We expanded further on Jung's theory of active imagination in our chapter on Dreams and Active Imagination (Chapter 6).

Fry (1974) discovered that various moods and conditions could be "worked through" in active imagination if the client would find a symbol from the unconscious for that mood or condition, then observe the autonomous development of the symbol while in a state of complete passivity and receptivity to what emerges from the unconscious. The active imagination process can then continue or be enhanced by painting or sculpting the symbols.

Jennifer

Jennifer was a fearful, but talented and delightful eleven-year-old girl who developed agoraphobia shortly after the death of her beloved grandmother. Her symptoms included the fear of overnight stays at friends' homes, the fear of eating out at restaurants, plus other fears which kept her from leading a normal pre-adolescent social life. These feelings, we concluded, were associated with the guilt that she felt because she had left home to stay overnight with her cousins the night that her grandmother died. As is often the case with survivor guilt, this child rationalized that her grandmother would not have died had she stayed at home.

During Jennifer's treatment, we used art and photography to help her deal with her loss. Jennifer began her work by drawing happy memories of being with her grandmother, times when they were doing things together. In one drawing, she drew a Christmas scene in which her grandmother was sitting in a chair by the tree. These drawings were bound into a memory album, which she could look at whenever she felt sad about her grandmother.

Jennifer was also invited to bring in photographs of her grandmother, especially photographs of the two of them together. These photographs helped Jennifer to recall more pleasant times they had together and the special bond that had developed between them.

During the course of Jennifer's therapy, she was able to venture out socially little by little. At first, she was encouraged to stay for only the early part of the evening when her friends were having sleep over parties. She was not to attempt any overnight visits. During her sessions, Jennifer was guided to attempt some risk-taking behavior progressively in her imagination. She became very successful in seeing herself, in her mind's eye, feeling comfortable and happy in situations that she would otherwise consider fearful. Gradually, Jennifer found that she was able to spend the night at the home of a close friend if, in the case of a panic attack, she knew her parents would be available to drive her home during the night. After several months, Jennifer not only felt confident enough to spend the night at a sleep over party, but she was able to dine out with her friends.

These grief therapy methods which focus on recalling memories of a deceased loved one are effective with both children and adults. Grief is one of the deepest of human emotions and is often overlooked as a problem for children, especially when the child's parents are consumed with their own grief. Often adults will spontaneously bring in photographs of a deceased family member in their attempts to resolve their grief issues. And, like Jennifer, the grief is often tinged with guilt; guilt for not having done enough, guilt for not having said enough, guilt for having said too much, guilt for not preventing the death, and the guilt of simply being a survivor.

The systematic desensitization that was used with Jennifer to help her to feel more comfortable on her sleep over trips away from home is commonly used with adults who suffer from intractable fears, such as the fear of crossing bridges, the fear of flying, or the fear of heights. In this behavior therapy treatment pioneered by Wolpe (1958), one's anxiety may be reduced by using relaxation as a counter-conditioning agent. In actual practice, patients or clients are guided by the therapist to imagine themselves as being confident and at ease as they progressively and in stages go through the mental mechanics of conquering their fears.

Jennifer came into the therapy session one evening with a bad dream. In the dream, Jennifer is shopping with her mother at a department store. Other customers in the store begin to act frightened and point towards the large plate glass window at the front of the store. Police cars have pulled up. Suddenly, Jennifer sees a spaceship hovering in the air. She wakes up in terror.

Our first step after describing the nightmare was for Jennifer to draw a picture of her dream. After completing her drawing, Jennifer agreed to continue the dream in active imagination using the Senoi people's method of dream work (see Chapter 6). She closed her eyes and repeated the dream again as if it were happening at that moment. Next, Jennifer gathered some allies and all of her courage to watch from the storefront as the spaceship landed. With trepidation, she inched closer to the spaceship as its doors opened. To her amazement and glee, out tumbled several colorful kitty cats. Cats, by the way, are the current love in Jennifer's life. When asked, "Is the dream frightening to you anymore?" Jennifer replied, "Not at all." She joyfully created another drawing with the cats coming out of the spaceship.

Unraveling the intricate patterns to Jennifer's fears took time and patience. One mystery was solved when Jennifer was able to talk about her misunderstanding of the word *alien*, which also led to more under-standing of her nightmare. Jennifer lives in Texas where newspaper headlines often tell of the large numbers of illegal aliens coming across the Texas border from Mexico. Illegal aliens were living in the community. They worked as gardeners, as household help, as carpenters, and in restaurants. Jennifer stayed on guard physically and psychologically with her fear that these aliens, in her mind *aliens from outer space*, lived among us, worked for us, served us our meals.

Fryrear had as a client several years ago a young man who related a misunderstanding he had had as a child. At age six, he had been riding in the back seat of the family car along a highway in Louisiana, bordered by bayous filled with floating water hyacinths. As he gazed at the plants, he simultaneously could smell a pervasive odor that filled the car. He said nothing but heard his parents talking about the odor, and his mother remarked that the odor was coming from the ammonia plant. The boy remembered that his aunt had died of pneumonia and misun-derstood the word "ammonia" for "pneumonia." He further assumed that the "plant" his mother mentioned was the floating plant in the bayou. The little boy became convinced, then, that the "pneumonia plants" filling the bayou were giving off an odor that would kill him. He tried to hold his breath the entire trip, about 20 miles, and was convinced for several years afterwards that the "pneumonia plants" would kill him with their odor.

Children often have unrealistic fears that are related to such misunderstandings, and the therapist must be alert for the possibility of such misconstruences. Children may be reluctant to mention such misunderstandings to their parents, and may suffer terrors in silence which show up as seemingly perplexing emotions or nightmares.

In addition to fear, other feelings such as guilt, loneliness, anger, and depression can be confronted or explored in photo art therapy. The client assumes a body pose which defines that mood or feeling. The artwork integrates the photography and elaborates the mood, often bringing about insight or resolution to the problem issue. The second step of identifying a contradictory feeling (calm or self-confidence instead of depression, for example) and posing to represent that feeling, along with a fantasy of acting out that feeling, can be very helpful in alleviating the distressing emotion.

Our final illustration is that of a child dealing with depression, brought about by his anxiety, and a possible prepsychotic split. For Jeremy, the feeling of sadness was overwhelming. His teacher noticed that he was not joining in with the other children and would, instead, sit alone, brooding. When his father brought Jeremy into treatment, he readily expressed his fear and reluctance to return to his mother's home for another summer visit. His two sisters also entered therapy when the time came closer for the summer visitation, and their dread began to escalate.

As it turned out, the summer visit was even more anxiety producing than anticipated. All three children were obviously afraid of their mother and her new husband, and all three returned to art therapy treatment in the fall. Eventually their father went to court and succeeded in curtailing visitation with the mother.

Some of Jeremy's artwork showed indications of a prepsychotic condition. Many of his images were leaning to one side; others were floating.

Jeremy complained of hearing voices in his head. One voice told him to steal money from his father's pocket; the other told him not to do it. He drew a picture of a face split in two. One side said, "Don't listen to the bad side;" the other said, "Don't listen to the good side." Such auditory hallucinations and art work are frequently indicative of premorbid schizophrenia.

Jeremy's favorite art therapy medium was sandplay. He had many battles between soldiers and dinosaurs and super heroes. During one session, I asked if *he* would like to be in the sand tray, in his scene in the sand. He agreed wholeheartedly. Jeremy posed for a picture which he pasted onto a small piece of poster board, then trimmed it. Next, we made a stand for his image with a small piece of poster board. When Jeremy set up his sandplay, he placed the good figures on one side of the tray and the bad figures on the other side. He, himself, was in the protective shadow of a giant black monster. Jeremy, always an active sandplay creator, played out the battle between the two opposing sides of the conflict. After engaging in and winning the battle in the tray, Jeremy appeared to be more calm and confident. His next role in the therapeutic process was to use the instant camera to photograph his sand tray, a copy for himself to take home and a copy for the files.

Figure 7-3. Jeremy and his two sides, the good and the bad.

Jeremy, in his own intuitive way, was attempting to bring together the divided aspects of his psyche. It was in this *temenos,* or protected container, that Jeremy was able to find the safety and freedom to explore and to overcome his greatest fears in a symbolic manner. In the following weeks, Jeremy's inner voices stopped and the leaning images in his art work straightened up. Several weeks later, Jeremy's father reported that he was busy in school and happy in his sports activities.

The sandplay that Jeremy used was the development of Jungian therapist Dora Kalff of Zurich, Switzerland (Kalff, 1980). The sand tray is made of plastic or wood. The tray ideally measures 19½″ × 28½″ × 3″ and is filled with sterilized sand. Miniatures, small figures, symbols, toys, etc., are made available to the sandplay artist to use in the sand tray. Children or adults can create scenes in the sand tray, which Kalff theorizes reflects the contents of the psyche. Kalff (1980, p. 29) writes that she gives the child's Self (or the center of the child's psyche), "the possibility of constellating and manifesting itself in therapy." She attempts, through the transference, to protect the child's Self and to stabilize the relationship between the Self and the ego. "This is possible within the psychotherapeutic relationship," Kalff continues, "because it corresponds to the natural tendency of the psyche to constellate itself at the moment when a *free and sheltered space* is created."

Adding one's photographic self-image to the sandplay scene is a recent development (Fryrear & Corbit, 1989). This personal stand-up figure brings the individual's own image into the tray to interact with other symbolic figures. The act of having the child's own image enter into the sandplay seems to lend a feeling of reality to the scene in the sand and allows the child to be personally involved in confronting his fears and resolving other conflictual issues.

We should emphasize here that the Polaroid Corporation warns against cutting into the instant photographs. To avoid any risks to children from the developing chemicals, we recommend that the therapist do the cutting, or that the photos not be trimmed.

Chapter 8

RESOLVING INTRAPSYCHIC CONFLICTS

There are conflicts between people and conflicts within people. Conflicts between people result in arguments, fights, guilt feelings, shame, anger, revenge, and a host of other feelings, actions, and experiences. Conflicts within result in arguments with oneself, fights with oneself, guilt feelings, shame, anger, revenge, and a host of other feelings, actions, and experiences. It is almost as if there are two people within the same body, arguing, fighting, trying to make each other feel anger, guilt, shame, or other feelings—trying to make each other do something, trying to manipulate, cajole, defend, expose. In this chapter, we are addressing conflicts within the person, rather than conflicts between people. We shall first refer to Jung's writing, describe types of conflicts, give some examples, and then show how photo art therapy can be useful in helping people to resolve conflicts.

Jung's theory of personality regards conflict as the rule, rather than the exception. In the Introduction, we alluded to Jung's concept of the tension of opposites. There is tension between conscious and unconscious elements in the psyche, each one compensating for the other. Another source of conflict, or tension, is the give and take between two attitudes, that of introversion and that of extraversion. The introverted attitude is turned inward, toward oneself, toward one's thoughts, emotions and memories. The extraverted attitude is turned outward, toward the external environment, particularly toward other people. The two attitudes are in more-or-less continual tension. The tension of opposites is inevitable and, in fact, is the source of energy for the psyche. It is also the root for a great number of psychopathological symptoms and the adoption of life styles that are not in the best interests of the person.

The tension of opposites energizes and propels a person along a life gradient, toward individuation. Unfortunately, there are a multitude of mistakes that can prevent a person from achieving true individuation. Jung has called these mistakes negative attempts to free the individuality. Briefly, these are a few of the negative attempts: One can become too rigid, refusing to see possibilities. One can adopt an extreme conscious attitude, to the exclusion of a more balanced personality. One can suddenly adopt the opposite attitude to one held previously, as in the well known mid-life crisis where a person suddenly turns his back on his previous life and strikes out in a new, opposite direction. One can remain in a state of conflict, and anxiety, for many months or years, stuck, as it were.

One can avoid these mistakes by taking a more positive approach. Jung called this positive attempt Individuation. "There is a destination, a possible goal, beyond the alternative stages dealt with in our last chapter (negative attempts to free the individuality). That is the way of individuation. Individuation means becoming a single, homogeneous being, and, in so far as 'individuality' embraces our innermost, last, and incomparable uniqueness, it also implies becoming one's own self. We could therefore translate individuation as 'coming to selfhood' or 'self realization'" (Collected Works, Vol. 7, page 171). We shall come back to individuation later in the chapter.

The concept of conflict has a long scholarly and literary tradition quite apart from Jung's writings. A modern attempt by Dollard and Miller (1950) to categorize conflict has become the standard classification system in psychology. In Miller and Dollard's model, there are three main types of conflicts, with several subtypes. There are approach-approach conflicts, avoidance-avoidance conflicts, and approach-avoidance conflicts. Approach-approach conflicts arise when a person is pulled in two directions simultaneously, and both goals have desirable outcomes. As a simple example, you are trying to decide between chocolate ice cream and vanilla ice cream. As a complex example, you are trying to decide which of two people to marry, and you love both equally well. Approach-approach conflicts rarely cause extreme anxiety or other debilitating emotions because you can't lose no matter what the outcome of the resolution. You still get the ice cream, you still marry someone you love.

Avoidance-avoidance conflicts arise when a person is confronted with two equally undesirable outcomes, and it is impossible to avoid both. No matter what the outcome, one of the alternatives will occur. For example, you have the choice of enduring a toothache or going to the dentist. Either way, you will experience some pain. Many young men during the Vietnam conflict were confronted with the choice of being drafted and facing combat, or fleeing the United States and becoming expatriates in Canada. Either choice led to far-reaching and undesirable consequences.

Certainly, avoidance-avoidance conflicts can lead to hardship and sadness, perhaps depression.

Approach-avoidance conflicts are the most likely to cause anxieties that are encountered in therapy. In an approach-avoidance conflict, one both desires and dreads the same outcome. You want to marry but you don't want to. You want to change jobs but you fear that you cannot find a better one. You want to move out on your own, but you dread having to make a living. Perhaps the most basic of approach-avoidance conflicts is that of taking a risk versus doing nothing. Nothing ventured, nothing gained — but nothing lost either. Many therapists have written about security versus risk taking. Sullivan (1953), for example, wrote about security operations, those activities, some pathological or self-defeating, that we engage in to ward off or avoid any possibility of risk in interpersonal relationships.

In the terminology of conflicts we are using here, the security versus risk taking is actually a double or multiple approach-avoidance conflict. Remaining secure and safe has both positive and negative consequences. Taking a risk has both positive and negative consequences. Consider the tragic but common experience of a battered wife. She can remain in the marriage and be financially secure but beaten. She can leave and be safe but penniless and on food stamps. And, of course, the consequences are much more complex and subtle than this simple-minded example. Most conflicts, in fact, are multiple conflicts, involving interwoven and mutually dependent outcomes, some known and some unknown.

When a person is "in conflict" that person is vacillating and ambivalent. Take the example of an approach-avoidance conflict. Bob is contemplating asking Janet, who works with him, to accompany him to the company picnic next Saturday. In his mind he contemplates all the known (to him) possible outcomes of his contemplated action. She will accept, they will fall in love, marry, have four children, divorce, hate each other, and end up in misery. She will laugh out loud and make derisive comments about his appearance in front of all the office. She will accept and then stand him up. He will start to ask her, and become tongue-tied and make a fool of himself. He will ask her, she will accept and they will have a wonderful time. The possibilities are bounded only by his imagination. The fact that many of the imagined disasters are improbable is of minor importance.

Because Bob is ambivalent, he puts off his decision. As Saturday nears, his conflict intensifies, and so does his anxiety. Eventually, he will escape the conflict in one way or another. He may make a decision and act on it.

Janet may ask him out. Janet may make the decision for him by accepting a date with George. Saturday may come and go while Bob is still trying to make up his mind. In this example, because the decision is time-bound, the conflict cannot last long. In many cases, however, there is no time limit and a person may remain in an agitated state of conflict for many days, weeks, or months. Often, our task as therapists is to help clients with the resolution of long-standing, gut-wrenching conflicts that have held them captive for many months, even years.

Why can't people resolve their conflicts without undue anguish? For one thing, they may not be able to see the conflict clearly. One side of the conflict, or even both sides, may be unconscious. They are not aware of all sides of the issue, and cannot make a suitable decision because all the facts are not available. For another thing, they may be exaggerating the probabilities of certain outcomes. Rather than thinking of a first date as a way to become acquainted, Bob is thinking far into the future about marriage, divorce, children, and who knows what else. Thirdly, people often set things up so that a certain outcome is practically guaranteed. Bob is convinced that Janet will reject him as a suitor, so he asks her out, not to the picnic, but to his place for the night. Because she hardly knows him, she refuses and he can then bask in the knowledge that he was right. He has then set the stage for further rejection and inappropriate propositions that lead to still further abasement. Because he has strong desires for heterosexual contact, his basic conflict is intensified and will continue to cause him severe anxiety.

People also keep conflicts alive so they won't have to experience the outcome, no matter what it is. Here the possibility of a tension of opposites between introversion and extraversion may come into play. The introversion attitude counsels thought and contemplation. The extraversion attitude counsels action. It is safer to live with anxiety than with action. Bob can agonize and daydream about Janet for his whole life, without ever taking her into his confidence. Fantasies are safe, but not very satisfying.

How can photo art therapy help? By providing a format for looking at all sides of a conflict. By making the outcomes tangible and concrete. By facilitating unconscious solutions. By helping the client see how he is engaging in self-defeating strategies and actions. By forcing, or at least encouraging, a metaphorical resolution of the conflict while in the safety of the therapy session.

Conflict Activity

As with most of the activities we have described, this one begins with a discussion. In this instance, the discussion is about conflicts, as described above. Clients are reassured that conflict is natural and inevitable and that everyone has conflicts. Nevertheless, the maintenance of a conflict without resolution for long periods of time takes a great deal of energy, energy that could be spent in more productive and exciting ways. Clients are asked to consider long-standing, fatiguing conflicts rather than frivolous or obviously temporary ones.

Having discussed and considered conflicts, the client then chooses one conflict to portray with the photographs and art. At this point in the assignment, clients are told to concentrate on how to depict the conflict, rather than how to resolve it. Many people are so concerned about the resolution that they want to jump ahead to that conclusion. One task of the therapist is to help the client work through the process slowly. The client is instructed to pose for photographs that would represent both poles of the conflict and the therapist (or group partner) takes the photos.

Using the photographs, other art media, and a poster board, the client makes a poster that depicts the conflict as clearly as possible. It is wise at this point in the art work to avoid using glue, because the client may want to move the parts of the poster.

Processing

With the poster as a guide, the client is told to reenact the poses used to portray both sides of the conflict. The client, in each pose, thinks of a one-word label for the pose. While maintaining the body pose, the client says the label out loud several times, shifting back and forth between the two poses and labels. The client is urged to pay particular attention to the body sensations and feelings that accompany the two poses and the changes from one to another. A common experience is for a memory from childhood to emerge suddenly during these movements, when one's body had experienced similar poses and the conflict at an early age. The therapist, too, can mirror the client's movements so as to become more empathetic. If in a therapy group, the entire group can move along with the client in a show of empathic support.

Still shifting from one pose to the other, the client is next instructed to change each pose very slightly in the direction of the other. And again, still another slight change, each pose in the direction of the other. When the poses begin to feel different from the original ones, the client is asked to think up new labels and to say them out loud. The point of this exercise is to approach some middle ground where the poles of the conflict can be seen not as incompatible opposites but as a tension of opposites that can be tolerated, transcended, and even appreciated. Eventually, the client will come to a point that feels comfortable or at least tolerable. The client then poses for a third photograph that can represent this middle ground. Sometimes, in very successful therapy sessions, the middle ground is not in the middle at all, but represents a new ground, a new, transformed perspective on the conflict.

The client adds the new, third photograph to the poster, while think-ing of ways the metaphorical conflict on the poster can be changed even more. Shapes can be altered. A color could be added. The relationships of the components could be changed by rearranging them. After the client and therapist have processed the piece thoroughly and the client is satisfied, everything can be glued down.

Harry

Harry was a forty-six year old man who took part in a photo art therapy program that included an assignment on conflict resolution. Most of the assignments and processing were done in pairs, with Harry and a partner helping each other. Harry's work on other assignments can be seen in Chapters 3, 6, and 9. During the conflict resolution assignment, he created the poster shown in figure 8-1.

Here are Harry's comments about the assignment:

> My partner and I talked about many different conflicts each of us had experienced; we tried to concentrate on ones that were a nuisance or were of a long-standing nature. Several conflicts came to mind, and I discarded some because they seemed too personal to share with my partner, and some because they seemed too difficult to get into at that time. It was not hard to think of conflicts. Apparently I have plenty of them. The hard part was deciding which one to work on first.
>
> Finally, I decided to try to understand better a long-standing habit I have of trying to keep many things going at once rather than concentrating on one thing at a time. On the one hand, I have heard the common wisdom of sticking with one task until it is finished and then going on to the next. On the other hand, there are always several things going on at once that need attention.
>
> I think I exaggerate the second to the detriment of the first. Often I wish I

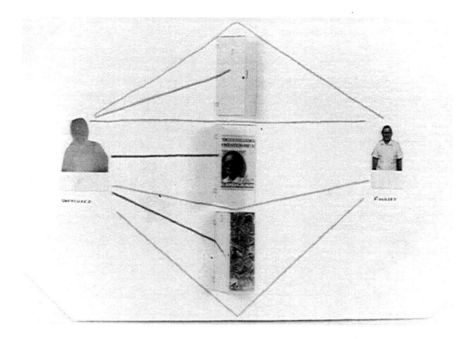

Figure 8-1. Harry's conflict and the three doors; love, fame and fortune, and adventure.

could be more concentrated, more focused on the task at hand rather than thinking about all the other things that are going on. Sometimes I feel like that circus performer who is balancing plates on poles, and who keeps adding more and more plates and poles while keeping all of the plates balanced at once.

In order to show the two sides of the conflict, I had my partner take my picture in focus (the focused side) and then out of focus (the unfocused side). The Polaroid cameras we were using could not be unfocused, so we put a piece of tissue over the lens so that the photograph would look unfocused. I did not change my pose for the two photographs because I feel like the same person whether I am focused or not. If I did it over again, I might show myself balancing several plates on one side and only one plate on the other.

After the photos developed, I placed them on opposite sides of a piece of poster board, not really knowing what else to do with them. My partner and I discussed the two poses, and I tried to stand and feel focused and unfocused. I remembered several instances of being unfocused and told my partner about them. For instance, I sometimes read three or four novels simultaneously. I might have one in the bedroom, another in the den, and still another on my desk in the office. At work, I often abandon one project to go to another, then back to the first. My desk looks like it too. I sometimes envy people who have a clean desk. No I don't. See, I am in conflict about it.

As we discussed the conflict, I suddenly remembered the television program that had the three doors. I think it was "The Price is Right." Contestants had to choose among three mystery doors that had prizes hidden behind them. It seemed to me that my focused-unfocused conflict was somehow tied in with mystery prizes, so I drew the three doors in the middle of the poster board and cut them out on three sides so they could be opened. I labeled them "1," "2" and "3" like on the television program.

It followed then that I should figure out what lay behind those doors, and why they were important in the poster. After thinking about it and talking it over with my partner, I have some ideas now. Behind door number one lies romance and love. You can't see it very well with the door partially closed, but I drew a red valentine and pasted it behind the door to represent love and romance. Behind door number two is fame and fortune. I pasted a dollar bill, with my picture instead of George Washington's on it, behind that door. Behind door number three is adventure. For that door, I took a picture of thick vegetation like in the jungle and glued it there.

I think that I am afraid, if I become too narrowly focused, that I will miss out on something. I might miss out on love, or fame and fortune, or adventure. If I remain unfocused, all possibilities are open to me. On the other hand, if I remain too unfocused, I can never really have a satisfying love life, make any money, or become famous. Being unfocused can be an adventure, but it can be dangerous and I could get lost.

When I first placed the two photographs on the poster board, I had the fantasy that I would work through the conflict and end up as a highly focused person. What actually happened was much different. As I talked about the photos and drew the doors, I became more and more comfortable with the whole idea of being somewhere in the middle, and the conflict gradually came to be less important to me. I discovered that I like being open to new possibilities, being unfocused. At the same time, my partner reminded me of times that I have been completely focused. As I think about it, there have been many times in my life when I have been able to concentrate on one thing for long periods of time. In other words, I don't have to be one or the other, I can be both. It is really a scheduling problem. I can schedule times when I can be completely focused, if necessary. As a reminder, I have the poster hanging on the wall in my office, next to my messy desk.

Harry's artwork and resulting dialogue and resolution illustrate very clearly Jung's statement, "The shuttling to and fro of arguments and affects represents the transcendent function of opposites. The confrontation of the two positions generates a tension charged with energy and creates a living, third thing—not a logical stillbirth in accordance with the principle *tertium non datur* but a movement out of the suspension between opposites, a living birth that leads to a new level of being, a new situation. The transcendent function manifests itself as a quality of conjoined opposites" (Collected Works, Vol. 8, p. 90).

Chapter 9

DEALING WITH APATHY AND DEPRESSION

L et us begin with a caveat. A major clinical depression is a very dangerous state to be in. It is estimated that 15 percent of people who are in a major depression attempt suicide. Because of the seriousness of depression, we should not overlook any treatment program that can offer quick and lasting relief. Two traditional methods, in particular, show promise in the treatment of depression. Antidepressant medication, the monoamine oxidase inhibitors and tricyclic iminodibenzine derivatives, can literally be lifesavers. It would be remiss of art therapists, or any other nonmedical therapists, to overlook the possibility that medication can be useful and even crucial in the treatment of depression. We should be open to the option of referring clients for possible prescription of such medications by a psychiatrist.

A second promising treatment program for depression is that of Aaron Beck, who has pioneered a cognitive-behavioral approach (see Beck, 1967, 1976; Beck, Rush, Shaw, and Emery, 1979). The cognitive-behavioral approach is somewhat removed theoretically from the ideas of Carl Jung. In particular, cognitive-behaviorism does not posit unconscious processes as central to a disorder. Rather, the cognitive-behavioral perspective concentrates on conscious "self talk" that the client uses to prolong and exacerbate the depressed state. We shall return to this topic later in the chapter.

It is even more important to consider medication in the treatment of manic-depressive disorder. Lithium is superior to any other treatment method in alleviating the severe mood swings experienced by manic-depressive disorder clients. There is mounting evidence that manic-depressive disorder has a strong heritability component and is most probably caused by a biochemical abnormality of some type.

With these cautions out of the way, we can proceed with a discussion of photo art therapy in the treatment of mood disorders. As an adjunct to these proven treatment methods, or as a primary method in the treatment of less severe mood disorders, photo art therapy can be of real benefit. Apathy, indecision and procrastination accompanied by "the blahs," and chronic dysthymic conditions, are all candidates for photo art therapy.

Jung (Collected Works, Vol. 7) made a distinction between "genuine melancholia" and psychogenic depression. In the case of melancholia, a person has fantasies of hopelessness, death and dying, helplessness, and passivity *because* she is depressed. But in the case of psychogenic depression, the opposite is true. The person is depressed because of the fantasies. The fantasies, in turn, are attempts on the part of the self to communicate to the ego that individuation has been blocked. It is psychogenic depression that can be treated analytically. The main thrust of the analysis is to help the client recognize the fantasies for what they are, attempts at inner communication from the unconscious to the conscious ego. The analyst therefore tries to help the client "stay with" the mood and to understand it. The client is advised to immerse herself in the depressive fantasies and images in order to understand them. Eventually, their meaning will become clear, and individuation can proceed.

Many clients become fearful of the power of their depression, and well they might. The mood can cause them to retreat from life, to become apathetic, immobile, and, sometimes, even self-destructive. Jung often used his active imagination technique (see Chapter 6) to work with depression, which, incidentally, is most successful with situational depression and should be used only by experienced therapists. The formal diagnostic category for situational or circumstantial depression is "Adjustment disorder with depressed mood" or "Adjustment disorder with mixed emotional features" (American Psychiatric Association, 1987, p. 331).

In the active imagination technique, which can be spontaneous or artificially induced, one can use a bad mood as a beginning and then allow one's fantasy images to appear, or watch for images that express one's mood. One concentrates one's attention on this image which as a rule will alter and become animated. Jung recommends that these alterations be noted for they reflect psychic processes in the unconscious. "In this way conscious and unconscious are united, just as a waterfall connects above and below" (Collected Works, Vol. 14, pp. 495–496).

As an example, Corbit had as a client, a man who was subject to periodic depressions. These bouts with depression caused him severe anguish both inter- and intrapersonally. Using active imagination the man was directed to focus upon an image that expressed his depressed mood, then to immerse himself into that image. He reported seeing himself going down a deep shaft. In his imagination, he continued down the shaft until he found himself blocked by a barrier of some sort. The barrier seemed impenetrable. Then, gathering all of his resources, he pushed through the blockage and discovered himself looking into a garage. He was asked to look around the garage in his imagination. As he looked about the garage, he could see two small boys throwing newly-born kittens against a clothes dryer. The kittens were now dead. He recognized the boys as himself and a little friend at the age of three. They were in his friend's garage. The young man wept as he told his story.

The client reported that his parents had never mentioned the incident, and that he had forgotten it until he was about fifteen or sixteen years old. It was around the time this memory returned that his bouts with depression began.

In a follow-up interview three years after treatment, the client reported that he had further bouts with depression after that insight, but the bouts were infrequent and less severe. He said that "there is more space between shame and myself." For this client, reaching into the depths of his depression and discovering its root helped him to deal realistically with this shame-based incident.

Childhood incest experiences that have been forgotten or repressed can be the cause of chronic shame-based depression, similar to our earlier case of the young man. In other cases of depression, the condition is created by an incident or series of incidents or the "meaningless" state of the client's life. The death or illness of a family member can cause depression that can last months or even years. The loss of a job or the "acting out" behavior of one's adolescent children are sometimes identified as causes of depression.

Artistic clients and students have reported to us that they often experience mood swings of depression and elation which appear to correspond to their creative endeavors. During the incubation, or pregnant phase of their creativity, artists often enter a state of depression; whereas, during the creation period, they usually experience a sense of excitement or elation.

Another recently-identified cause of depression is seasonal light deprivation (seasonal affective disorder). For some people the lack of sunlight during winter months creates a sense of hopelessness, apathy, and depression in them.

It is not uncommon for clients to suffer a depressed state which occurs at the same time year after year. When this "anniversary" condition is reported, we ask, "What happened to you at this time of the year in the past?" The answer is usually one of amazement: "Oh, my mother died five years ago at this time" or "I miscarried a baby in late July and now I get depressed every year at this time." A veteran reported that he experienced severe cyclical depression every year in mid-March. When he was asked, "What happened to you in mid-March in your past?" he quickly replied, "Oh, that was the time of the Tet Offensive in Vietnam. Many of my buddies were killed then."

One client who suffered from cyclical depression painted a startling portrait of a black man over a weekend in early March several years ago. The painting was unlike anything that she had ever done before. It was realistic and detailed, whereas, customarily, her paintings were abstract. The background was painted in blood red. The woman reported that she had been extremely depressed for several days, then felt compelled to paint. When asked about what, if anything, had happened in the past at this time of the year, she replied, "Oh, I guess I haven't told you, I was raped in early March eight years ago." She had unintentionally painted her attacker. Her shame about the rape had caused her to suppress the incident, which her unconscious later, through the painting, forced into her consciousness. This spontaneous active imagination process helped her to begin to work on her issues and to let go of her cyclical depression.

Another woman in her mid-forties who was suffering from depression and a sense of "meaninglessness" in her life used clay to express this depressive mood. She worked for several hours putting her mood into the clay, sculpting a woman whose head was bowed down, deep into despair. She was totally drawn into the process, almost as if the process had overtaken her. After completing the sculpture, she felt overwhelmed by words of a poem that filled her head. She put the words on paper.

DESPAIR

Despair, no longer can I deny your existence.
For ages, I pushed away all thoughts of you,
Refusing your messages,
My false gaiety keeping you at a distance.
And yet you thrived, Despair.
You twisted my body;
You tore at my stomach;
You rumbled through my bowels demanding attention.

I could feel you in the marrow of my bones, Despair,
Wanting me to acknowledge you,
Calling to me in dreams,
Beckoning, beckoning me to unite with you.
Despair, at last you've won.
I accept our coniunctionis.
The numbness is gone—
I experience you in all your dark splendor.
Despair, we are one.

The author of the poem discussed how she felt a sense of meaninglessness in her life and, in a way, had lived through the lives of her husband and children. She had attempted to stay cheerful and "up" for friends and family, yet refused to look at the depressive feelings that nagged at her. After she worked on her clay piece, she said, "It was as if I was in touch with the despair of the world, and it all went into that piece of clay. I was connected. I was despair. And that piece just emerged."

In continuing her therapeutic work using clay and active imagination, our poet sculpted another figure of a woman. Again the figure was depressed looking, with bowed head. And again, a poem intruded upon her:

STRUGGLE

From the depths of the clay
    she came,
As if she always knew
    she would be born.
Initially, her face appeared,
    already formed.
There was no question
    of her cry for release.
Swiftly, I pulled the clay
    from her body,
Afraid for her fragile life.
We worked in unison, we two:
She, demanding to be born,
I, the obedient midwife.
Later, I smoothed her body,
    Running my hands
    Down her spine,
    Caressing her buttocks.
Then we sighed
Like two spent lovers;
And it was good.

This time the woman was able to acknowledge some positive results from her work. The depression had begun to lift and she was able to perceive a more global view of her life. She reported that finding these artistic outlets helped her to express her feelings and moods in a more creative and less self-destructive manner. The active imagination method of using the expressive arts to work on a dream, or, as in this case, on a depressed mood, is described more fully by Jung (Collected Works, Vol. 8):

> It does not suffice in all cases to elucidate only the conceptual context of a dream-content. Often it is necessary to clarify a vague content by giving it a visible form. This can be done by drawing, painting, or modelling. Often the hands know how to solve a riddle with which the intellect has wrestled in vain. By shaping it, one goes on dreaming the dream in greater detail in the waking state, and the initially incomprehensible, isolated event is integrated into the sphere of the total personality, even though it remains at first unconscious to the subject.
>
> Once the unconscious content has been given form and the meaning of the formulation is understood, the question arises as to how the ego will relate to this position, and how the ego and the unconscious are to come to terms. This is the second and more important stage of the procedure, the bringing together of opposites for the production of a third: the transcendent function. At this stage it is no longer the unconscious that takes the lead, but the ego (pp. 86–87).

From another Jungian perspective, Carolyn Fay, dance therapist at The C. G. Jung Educational Center in Houston, Texas, uses active imagination and dance/movement to work with various moods and emotional states. Using music to guide the mood, she directs students to use their bodies to express their feelings. The student's active imagination process continues spontaneously in movement, then is processed in the dance/movement group.

Now back to the cognitive-behavioral treatment of depression. Briefly, the approach developed by Beck and his colleagues involves, as its name implies, both cognitive and behavioral strategies. The cognitive part of the therapy can be broken down simplistically into four phases. Phase One seeks to help the client identify self-defeating pessimistic thoughts that occur more or less automatically and that serve to keep the person feeling defeated, hopeless, and depressed. Examples of such thoughts are "I will never find a good job again," "Nobody loves me and I am unlovable," or "I am doomed to unhappiness forever."

Phase Two of the therapy is to help the client see the connection between the self-defeating cognition and the depression. By remembering the places and times when these automatic thoughts occurred, clients can see that their depressed mood deepened after such thoughts. Having clients keep a log (a behavioral strategy) of pessimistic thoughts and the accompanying mood helps them to see the connection.

Phase Three is to carry out an objective, realistic, logical analysis of the automatic thoughts to see if there is, in fact, any objective evidence for the beliefs. One result of such an analysis is that clients begin to see that words such as "never," "nobody," and "forever" are simply not logically defensible. The automatic thoughts of *never* finding a job, *nobody* loving me, and unhappy *forever* cannot be logically defended, they can only be defended at the expense of logic and realism.

The fourth phase of the cognitive therapy is to help the client replace the automatic, illogical, and unrealistic thoughts with more realistic ones. The statement, "I will never find a good job again" can be replaced more realistically with "It takes time and effort to find the job I prefer." The statement, "Nobody loves me and I am unlovable" can be replaced with statements like, "Some people like me, and as I make more of an effort to be a friend, more people will like me and love me." The statement, "I am doomed to be unhappy forever" can be restated more realistically as "Right now I am unhappy but as my mood improves and as I make friends, I will feel better."

Beck believes that cognition is not enough, and that clients need to act. Accordingly, clients are given assignments to keep lists of automatic thoughts, to fill out rating forms such as the Beck Depression Inventory (a 21-item rating scale), and to schedule activities that have a high likelihood of resulting in pleasurable consequences. Social skills training is also frequently a part of the behavioral component in the therapy.

How can photo art therapy augment such a cognitive-behavioral program? At first glance, the two approaches seem incompatible, but they are not. Cognitions are not only words, they are also images. Many experiences, especially early preverbal experiences, must be encoded and stored in the memory as visual images rather than mediated as words. Even later experiences that are translated into words and stored in that form may have visual images concomitant with the experience. Theoretically, there is no reason why there cannot be automatic images as well as automatic words. Many of these images, it seems to us, would be more or less unconscious or at least not consciously recognized by the clients as tied to a particular mood. Jung, in fact, mentions just such an example. One of his clients had an image of his fiance jumping into a fissure of a frozen lake while he stood by helplessly. Jung describes such images and accompanying feelings of the man as "so many auto-suggestions which he accepts without argument" (Collected Works, Vol. 7, p. 212).

Beck's approach, which concentrates on self-talk, ignores the nonverbal, imagery component. It seems obvious to us that a cognitive treatment approach to depression can and should incorporate images along with words in the therapy program. Such a program would meld elements of Jung's concepts with those of Beck, possibly leading to a more effective approach to the treatment of depression than either alone.

Buchalter-Katz (1989) reports on the use of directed art therapy with hospitalized depressed patients. She asked patients to draw obstacles to recovery, that is, the barriers that the patients throw up to prevent them from functioning better than they are. In most cases the patients could quickly and boldly draw such barriers, which represent images having to do with feelings of hopelessness and helplessness. The images, as drawn by the patients, contained many symbols of barriers. They used heavy pressure, black or dark colors, spirals, walls, and fragmented and unconnected lines. Clearly the patients' images associated with the depression were readily available to the patients and they had no difficulty drawing them. Buchalter-Katz remarked on the rapidity with which the patients began and completed the art assignments. One could speculate that the images were begging for recognition, crying out to communicate with the ego, as Jung hypothesized.

Just as people have a rich and varied verbal repertory they also have a rich and varied imaginal repertory. Just as each person has a uniquely individual verbal repertory, each person has a uniquely individual imaginal repertory. Paralleling the four phases of cognitive-behavioral therapy listed above, then, the photo art therapist would fashion a four-phase imaginal-creative program.

The photo art therapist would first help a person to be aware of her own pessimistic or self-defeating images. Such images would be unique for each person and would have to come from the person. According to the work of Buchalter-Katz, such images would likely be barriers of some sort.

Secondly, the therapist would help the client discover the connections between the images and the mood. It seems likely to us that the connections between the images and the mood would be more easily discovered and accepted by the clients than the connections between words and mood because there would be less chance of interference by verbal defenses such as rationalizations, blaming others, or intellectualization.

The third phase of Beck's treatment, attacking the self-talk on logical grounds, would not be possible with the images. However, it would be possible to attack the images on metaphorical grounds, to examine if the symbolic meanings of the images are, in fact, congruent with the more realistic facts. For example, if the image was one of being hopelessly bound by chains or locks, symbolic of feelings of helplessness, that image could be examined from the point of view of how helpless the client really is in various spheres of life.

The last phase of a photo art therapy program that parallels Beck's cognitive approach would be to replace the self-defeating images with more uplifting, self-promoting ones. Using the example of chains and locks, the person could imagine breaking the chains or finding the combinations or keys to the locks.

Buchalter-Katz, although not specifically relating her work to the more cognitive work of Beck, was carrying out a program very much like his. She reports that, after the patients had drawn the images of depression, she would have them discuss the characteristics of the images and how they could be changed. In small groups, the patients would discuss whether the images were insurmountable, to what extent the barriers could be undermined, broken through, or climbed over. The goal of the group art therapy was to help the patients find "methods of dealing with the barrier and overcoming it" (p. 360).

The photo art therapy approach to apathy and depression is similar to that reported by Buchalter-Katz, with the addition of photographs and somewhat more extensive direction. We begin by having the clients pose for a photograph that represents how they are preventing themselves from living a more fulfilling life. Like Jung, we have the client imagine himself being immersed in the pessimistic mood and imagine how that is presenting a barrier to a happier mood state. If the client has carried out the "visual transitions" exercise (see Chapter 11) that portrays how he is now on the one hand, and how he wants to be on the other, that poster can be used as a beginning point for this activity. Using the "visual transitions" poster, we can ask directly how the client prevents himself from making the transition from one pose to the other. We bring in at this point a discussion of verbal self-talk that is likely associated with the images and the mood. Such self-defeating and blocking statements as "I'm just not smart (or lovable, or strong, or young) enough" are offered as examples and similar self-defeating statements are elicited from the client, just as in the Beck program.

When the client is ready, we have him pose in a self-defeating way and take his picture. The client is then instructed to make a poster of the depressed, blocked state using the photograph and any other art materials available. Freeflowing black and colored paint or marking pens should be a part of the art materials provided for depressed clients, as well as tissue paper and construction paper which includes black and brown as well as colors. If the activity takes place in small groups, we have the people work in pairs so that they can take each other's picture and help each other with the poses.

With the finished poster in front of him, we ask the client to elaborate on the poster, and the metaphorical significance of it, just as Buchalter-Katz does with the art work prepared by her depressed patients. We then adopt a more cognitive approach, and instruct the client to come up with three reasons how the self-defeating pose prevents him from moving to a more adaptive pose. The purpose of this instruction is to help the client see the relationship between the image and the mood of helplessness and hopelessness.

Following the discussion of the helplessness and hopelessness inherent in the poster, we then ask the client to decide on three ways that he *can* move out of the pose depicted in the poster. In other words, how can the image be changed in a metaphorical way? When the client, with the help of the therapist, can state how the poster could be changed, he is then encouraged to do so, with whatever other photographed poses or art work that are needed. The goal of the therapy is to change the image to a more positive, adaptive one, just as the goal of Beck's therapy is to change to more positive, adaptable self-talk.

Harry

Harry is a 46-year-old man who has experienced cyclical depression from time to time throughout his life. There is a history of manic-depressive illness in his family, although Harry has never experienced the severe mood swings that characterize that disorder. His periods of depression have always been rather mild and he has never been unable to work or to carry out his daily routine. He has had periods when he felt like crying for no particular reason and when he felt listless and apathetic. He has been in brief psychotherapy twice and experienced some relief each time. Harry took part in an extensive photo art therapy program which included a segment having to do with depressed mood. Other examples of Harry's work during the photo art therapy program are reproduced and discussed in Chapters 3, 6 and 8.

During the present assignment, Harry completed the poster shown in Figure 9-1. He depicted the depressed state first, at the bottom of the poster, and then added the top figures and the rainbow later. He described the assignment as follows:

It seems to me that when I am in a dejected mood, it is like being mired up to my knees in mud, or in a swamp. I feel heavy and weak, and my body is slumped over. If I try to move, it is like dragging my feet through black, gooey ooze. I posed for a picture of myself slumped over in a passive, nonmoving stance. I cut my image out of the photograph and then planted it firmly in the middle of a circular swamp, using a black crayon to show the heavy viscosity of the swamp ooze. I also drew in an echo of that pose and the black surroundings using the negative of the photograph and a gray crayon to show that the depressed state starts out mild and progresses to a more dejected state. Or sometimes it never progresses beyond a mild "gray" funk.

I can't seem to move from that pose because of the terrible effort required. I can't move because that would require that I raise my head up and look around, and that is too much trouble. I can't move because movement would disturb the ooze and that somehow can't or shouldn't be done. I am stuck there, pathetic and apathetic. It seems like I might stay there forever.

In my real life, I get stuck by procrastinating or by withdrawing into myself. I am aware that my face freezes so that I don't show any emotion and that I cannot seem to say to other people what I am feeling. When I am by myself I feel sad. Sometimes I hear a sad song or see a sad movie and begin crying. If other people are around I try not to let on that I feel like crying. As a matter of fact, I am a little embarrassed right now just admitting it. Usually I can break out of that mood by working.

These episodes come on me about once a year, or sometimes more often for brief periods of a day or two. It seems to me that I am especially vulnerable in the spring of the year, about April or May. I don't know why. The episodes don't last very long, maybe a week or two at a time. They have never been so severe that I felt like giving up, but I have felt like escaping. The escape fantasy always takes the form of going off by myself someplace.

How can I get out of the slump? First I have to hold my head up and move my arms around. Some music would help. I love to dance and music would help me get moving. And some color. All this blackness needs to be replaced with color. I think that music, movement and color are the answer. I tried to show that by drawing a colorful rainbow arching over the swamp and placed another picture of myself walking along, supported by the colors of the rainbow and whistling a tune. My head is held high and I am cheerful. This

Figure 9-1. Harry in a slump, and "movin' on out."

image is a happy one for me. I used the negative of this pose to show that, ideally, the happy mood would extend into the future.

I notice that there are no other people in my poster. That is surprising to me. I like to be around other people except when I am in a funk, yet I did not include them when I changed my poster. There is a glimmer of an insight there for me, but I don't get it yet. I think it has something to do with my reluctance to rely on other people, they may let me down. I have a fantasy of someone pulling me out of the swamp, then at the last moment letting me fall back in.

Now that I look at the swamp and the rainbow, it occurs to me that the rainbow is a bridge over the swamp, and that, if I could plan ahead sufficiently, I could stay on the bridge and out of the swamp altogether. I need to learn more about that bridge.

Note that Harry first drew an image representative of his depressed mood, the circular swamp. The swamp, with its clinging mud, can be seen as a barrier, similar to the images drawn by Buchalter-Katz's clients. Secondly, he was able to make three statements as to why or how he was unable to progress beyond the barrier, and to relate that to his real life. The third phase of the therapy was for Harry to identify more positive statements and a more positive metaphorical image, and to attack the first image on logical grounds. He was able to identify music and dance as real-life instances when he was not, in fact, "mired down." The last phase of the art therapy for Harry was to imagine a more uplifting scene and to depict that, in his case the rainbow image.

There are two obvious parallels between Harry's "swamp" poster and his picture of one of his dreams (see Chapter 6) and the accompanying active imagination. In Harry's dream, he was wading through sticky mud, similar to the swamp depicted in the poster in this chapter. In the active imagination process, Harry emerged from the mud onto firm ground and remarked, "Now I can walk a little more jauntily . . . Maybe I'll start whistling or something like that, or singing," strikingly similar to his depiction of the rainbow and music in the poster shown above. One can assume that Harry's dream and Harry's "swamp" poster are both depictions of unconscious images associated with depression. In both instances, his conscious attempt to deal with the depressing images was to move, to walk, and to turn to music.

Chapter 10

NURTURING THE HURT CHILD WITHIN:
A CASE STUDY

Unexpected and unsolicited information in the form of art images often emerges from the photo art therapy work of students and clients. This information can be data of a personal nature, which has been long denied or repressed in the unconscious psyche or it can be knowledge of a more universal nature from the collective unconscious or collective psyche. In regards to the art images from the personal unconscious, Jung would say that this is subjective art which draws its contents from "inside." He contended that the unconscious psyche affects consciousness through its pictorial elements, so he often encouraged his patients to draw their dreams or these images from inside. Subjective images are recognizable as subjective and personal because they do not correspond to any external reality (Collected Works, Vol. 15).

Judith

In the following case study, images from the personal unconscious came forth in the student's artwork which reinforced some of her recent personal therapy work. Her early traumatic experiences had been repressed for years. Then, through her therapy she was able to acknowledge her past and begin to work through her denial of the circumstances. Her confrontation of the past through her powerful art images again stirred the dreadful memories, but offered her the avenue to come to terms with them.

From the first day of our summer photo art therapy class, it was obvious that Judith, a petite and attractive woman, was dealing with oppressive sadness. Fortunately for Judith, she joined the most extraverted of our two classroom groups, a group in which she developed enough trust to share both the depth of her despair and her capacity for joy.

The setting for the class was ideal for photo art therapy: a wooded conference site on the shores of Lake Geneva, Wisconsin. The twelve students who had signed up for the course provided an ideal class size, too. The environment was conducive to creativity, relaxation, and a shift in consciousness allowing a new perspective to evolve on both worldly and personal problems.

Judith's first piece of work for the class was her *Visual Transitions* ("As I Am" and "As I Would Like To Be") project (see Chapter 11). She created two separate pictures. The "As I Am" picture (Figure 10-1) shows her cut-out image in the center of a tree with branches extending from either side of her. She appears to be struggling in a black web-like setting. On the left side of the picture, the background of the photograph is seen impregnated into the dead tree branches. On the right side, the branches have some greenery and three sun-like yellow spheres appearing at the tops of the branches.

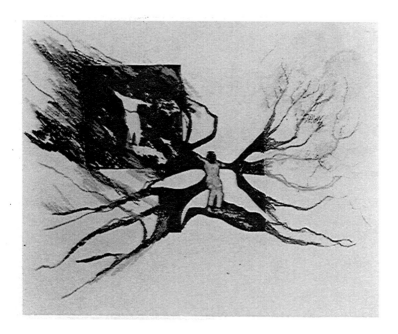

Figure 10-1. Judith's self-portrait, "As I am."

In her second art piece, the "As I Would Like To Be" picture (Figure 10-2), Judith has drawn a young woman's face colored primarily in blue and purple. The woman has a dream-like visage. The left side of the woman's face is composed of spirals of yellows and greens. Judith placed a photograph of herself in the center of the woman's forehead. She portrays herself this time in a relaxed position between two trees. The branches of the trees integrate with strands of hair on the young woman.

Figure 10-2. Judith's self-portrait, "As I would like to be."

Judith's summary of her first day's *Visual Transitions* project is as follows:

In the first session, we were asked to take two photographs: "Me as I am" and "Me as I would like to be."

In the first one I thought of myself as trying to pull together two parts of myself that I so successfully split apart early in my life. In the photo itself, I found two limbs from separate trees, wrapped my arms around them and pulled hard. I felt it was impossible to join them! As I created the background, I saw (Again! I've been working on this for a while) the opposite poles of me—my feelings of darkness, rage, pain, despair, trauma, and horror separate from a playful, happy, gentle, positive me. I named this picture: "I've GOT to do this!"

Myself as I'd like to be was portrayed standing between two limbs of a strong, stable tree—leaning, relaxed. I placed this photo in the middle of my forehead, and in the face were all the colors of my previous struggle. I hope to come to an integration of myself, finally embracing ALL of who I am. I named this "I'm okay."

In the group process, as I took my first position and had a person on each side pull away from me, I felt the pain of my intense struggle. I appreciated the understanding I received as others assumed the pose. I realized that maybe it would be easier if I didn't pull so hard! A more relaxed position could be more beneficial.

The second day's assignment was to focus on a conflictual problem and to pose for photographs representing the opposite poles of the conflict (see Chapter 8). Judith's picture incorporated both parts of her conflict into the one project (Figure 10-3). The picture is fragmented and eerie, composed of torn pieces of paper in reds and blacks; an impression is created of a fire in the night. Judith placed herself in a doorway on the left side of her picture, behind a screen. She added a streak of red paint which seems to penetrate her lower body, giving the illusion of fire or a rocket. Judith also placed herself into the doorway on the right. She is more open and vulnerable in this scene. Steps go up to the doorway, but one set of steps doesn't quite reach the doorsill. There are other stairs in the picture, but they, too, don't seem to go anywhere.

Judith says:

On the second day we were to pose in positions that showed two sides of a conflict. I wanted to convey my conflict as the protective shield that doesn't allow good or bad to enter too deeply—at this time, especially good. Part of me is frightened by the possibility of someone getting too close. In believing and really receiving positive feedback, I may be opening myself to some kind of abuse—something that I had experienced before and so carefully protected myself from as I grew up. I see it as a conflict now, not allowing me to absorb the goodness in myself as I receive that message from others. The first photograph was easy. I am behind a closed door. My face is barely visible and my hands are in a position of self-defense. The next picture never seemed ade-

Figure 10-3. Judith in conflict.

quate until the third attempt—lying in the sun in the midst of absorbing shadows.

The most difficult part of this exercise was depicting these poses artistically. The third photo that I wanted to use to portray the resolution to my conflict just didn't seem to fit. Neither did the second. I found myself using black and red photos from magazines, and pictures of steps, along with the first picture I took to show a resolution—my least favorite one. I am standing in an open doorway with steps leading to the interior, but it didn't seem adequate to me! The black and red and stairwells have a painful significance to me of the same trauma that caused the protective shield to be formed. I really wasn't planning on including that aspect of my conflict. I decided to use the other photos on a second sheet—at least that is where I hope to be someday—obviously it's too early now. I had a headache at the end of the creative process, and was relieved when I didn't have to share my work with the group. I felt too vulnerable at that time and was unclear about the meaning of my work. I just knew that it hurt deep down inside.

Even though the assignment called for Judith to simply look at both sides of the conflict, she took it further and attempted to resolve the conflict artistically.

For many students, the most difficult, yet most rewarding, exercise in this series is *Who am I in relationship to my shadow?* (see Chapter 4). One of the students in our class argued that, "If you recognize your shadow, it is no longer shadow." But to understand the Jungian concept of shadow one needs more than to recognize shadow. One needs to identify shadow, acknowledge shadow, work with shadow, play with shadow, and, lastly, integrate shadow. Shadow can be glimpsed and recognized through projections and nightmares. It can be identified through projections onto other people of the same sex, an emotional response either positive or negative to that other person.

The class was asked to pose for two photographs for this exercise: one was of a shadow aspect of themselves, the "Not I;" the other was to represent their egos, the "I" part of themselves. Judith's work was a study in contrasts. Her shadow aspect of herself was on the left side of the poster board. She was dressed in red, teeth bared, mouth wide open, assuming a frightening pose. The reds and blacks, reminiscent of her "Conflict" picture, appeared again in this picture. Judith's upper body is emerging from a hole within the network of black and red streaks.

Red and blue vein-like lines radiate from the picture on the right. Judith is at the center of a garden of flowers, smiling and contented. The scene on the right side of the picture is a dramatic contrast to the blacks and reds on the left. Using these red and blue vein-like lines, Judith has erected a partial circle around the ego aspect of herself. Judith herself referred to the right-hand photo as her persona (Figure 10-4).

Judith continues:

On the third day we were asked to portray our shadow and our persona. I thought immediately of my dark, angry side as shadow—some part of myself that I negate and have a hard time owning, and I thought of my delightful, colorful, pleasant self as my persona. I found this exercise most revealing! I enjoyed depicting my shadow in the photo and creating an appropriate background. I saw the persona as somewhat disgusting and unreal—too saccharine and flowery. I realized later that I was again doing a great splitting, only this time taking the side of the darkness. Both sides, of course, were already shown in the first project.

The most helpful part of this exercise was the small group interaction that followed. I felt the affirmation and acceptance of each person, so I was able to tell them my most hidden secret, and I found great release in screaming with

Figure 10-4. Judith's Shadow and Persona.

them—just as I was doing in my shadow photo! The session was very helpful to me—something I had been working toward in therapy. It was a small step, I suppose, but it seemed major to me.

The class worked hard on their shadow aspect, and many class members reported that they accomplished some important work which helped them to better understand Jung's concept of "shadow."

The following assignment was less emotionally charged. We asked the group to photograph one another in poses which describe *Who am I in relationship to nature?* (see Chapter 1).

Judith's poster was a cool study in blues. Her poster (Figure 10-5) contained four photographs of herself. In the top center photograph she is dressed in a long white dress and has her hands raised to the skies. In her second pose, just to the right of the "worshipping" figure, she is seated in a tree. The third pose, at the lower left, shows her playing in the water. Judith's fourth pose appears to be more oppressive because in this scene she is covered by the rocks.

According to Judith's description of her work:

Figure 10-5. Judith's relationship to nature.

On the fourth day the photos were to be an expression of myself with nature: Who I am in relation to earth, water, plants, and sky. This exercise was delightful to me and a kind of a celebration after the release of the previous day. Nature has always meant a lot to me—more recently it has BEEN me—something stable—something that IS, that I am a part of, and that no one can take away. I wanted to get as close to the elements in my pictures as I could—I wanted to BE the rocks, the soil, the foliage, and the water. I wanted to let the sky engulf me. I feel that in nature is the mystery of life and death and rebirth. It is so akin to my own journey. I wanted to be immersed and cleansed by the water—to be open and naked there, but felt somewhat inhibited in a public setting. The sky seemed like a symbol of the spirit within me that will never die.

The whole project was such a good experience! It was an integrating one and gave me a sense of rootedness. In the group interaction I felt some hesitation since my approach to this project seemed to be on a different level than the others. I learned that my approach didn't really matter—everyone seemed so receptive and affirming—something I needed to receive and cherish within me.

The "Nature" exercise points to the importance of listening closely to the artist's interpretation of her work. Observers of Judith's work might view the scene of "Judith under the rocks" to be symbolic of being weighted down, oppressed, buried, unable to move. But Judith describes her relationship with the rocks as wanting to "be" the rocks. Her description takes the "weightiness" away from the scene. However this would also be a time for Judith to listen to the projections of others upon her work. Is she overburdened or carrying the load of too many of her own or others' problems? Is she denying those aspects of her life? She might want to reappraise her interpretation and attend to what her unconscious has to say in her work.

Our last exercise for the course was designed to pull together the week's work, to look at what had happened, and to attempt to integrate these symbols and messages. Judith's work was a delight (Figure 10-6)! The left side of her picture again is dominated by reds and blacks. She has used positives and negatives artistically to represent the split which she described earlier in the week. Moving to the right, she has used two photographs of herself torn into two parts, one right side up, the other upside down. In one photograph Judith's face has closed eyes; in the other her eyes are open. In arranging the photographs, Judith separated them to put one closed eye and one open eye together, forming a more complete, or integrated, concept of self.

Continuing to the right, Judith posed for a picture on the boat dock. The photograph expresses a confident, happy woman. In the scene in the upper right corner, Judith has her arms open to the elements, framed as if on a stage. One might imagine her to be saying, "Here I am! This is me!" In fact, printed messages under the photograph read, "Born to reveal the woman you've become," and "Feel like a work of art."

The lower right corner contains a magazine picture of a young girl. The child looks as though she is ready to engage in a playful pillow fight.

And maybe Judith is ready at this time to take on the world in a more playful, assertive manner. Scenes in the collage are connected with blue and red ribbon-like streamers, reminiscent of party decorations.

Figure 10-6. Judith "pulls it all together."

As Judith describes her work:

On the fifth and last day, we were asked to look at the work we had done throughout the week and to pull it together, if possible, or to look at some transition point and what had happened. I had my partner take two pictures of my face, one with my eyes closed, the other open. I draped a blue cloth over my shoulders. In the other photos I wanted to depict my inner sense of excitement and integration, and I danced in the woods and sat near the water to absorb the sun and breeze. When I created the background, I unconsciously integrated the red, black, and blue colors that are symbolic of my journey. In some way the pain and rage and deep sorrow spilled over into the joy and enhanced it, and flowed back again to enrich the former area of darkness. It helped me to see an integration of the split. The words on the collage: "Born to reveal the woman you've become" and "Feel like a work of art" seemed to

express my inner wish (and belief). This expression was a rewarding experience for me—to say the least!

In the group process as I looked over each piece, explained it briefly, and
shared the final work, I could see even better what had happened in the week.
I think the group could see it, too—they clapped for me in acknowledgement
of my own sense of growth!

I came to this experience with an open heart to receive whatever might be
there for me. I learned that a stance of receptivity is very important in the
growth process. It took a long, long time to come to this point, however. I want
to remember the risk I was able to take, the pay-off for me, and this "safe place"
with others that I found. I also have the visual reminder of an integration that
is taking place in me—THAT is very hopeful!

In the brief period of one week, Judith not only learned a new therapy
method using art and photography as catalyst, but she worked through
some deep and painful issues for herself. Not every student could repli-
cate the process of Judith's work. Not every student had issues as deep
and penetrating as hers. In addition, Judith was ready and receptive to
working on issues which had interfered with her becoming her authentic
self—now she is ready to play, to take on the world with a pillow fight.

In a July, 1991, update on Judith's progress, four years later, she
reports that she has made some major changes in her life. She has
changed professions to one less structured. She is also deeply involved
with her art. Recently, in fact, she achieved a long-time dream when she
had a gallery showing of her art.

In recent years, art therapists have, through research and shared
observations, been able to recognize similarities in the images and symbols rendered by patients and clients who have experienced life-threatening
trauma (Spring, 1985; Cohen and Phelps, 1985; Sidun & Rosenthal,
1987). Spring (1985) conducted her doctoral research on indicators of
sexual abuse. She found that images of wedges and eyes were frequently
drawn by both rape and incest survivors. Cohen and Phelps (1985)
studied the art of child incest victims, and found that red houses, phallic-
looking trees, faces in clouds and trees, a face colored in, and one
window on a house which is different, in addition to other specific
images, could be indicators of child sexual abuse. Art therapists at study
group sessions at the American Art Therapy Association national confer-
ences have shared information on universal indicators of abuse, such as
sexualized figures, stairways, and thrusting objects in drawings.

It is not uncommon for clients who have been incest or sexual abuse
victims or victims of other traumas to have denied or repressed the

knowledge of their pain until psychotherapy or new or additional trauma triggers flashbacks or fragmented memories of their experiences. Today's therapists are more attuned to the possibilities of repressed trauma in their patients, and are better able to help their clients deal with these emotional factors than previously. At the present time, therapists, and especially art therapists, are more keenly aware of the visual symptoms and symbols expressed by trauma victims, whether they be rape or incest victims, combat veterans, or victims of other life-threatening situations. The artwork of these posttraumatic stress disorder clients not only aids in identifying the victims, but also helps these people to work through and overcome the pain that they have denied or hidden away in the unconscious for years (Corbit, 1985).

With regard to Judith's work, her personal interpretation of her artwork was of primary importance. Through the use of her art projects and the help of her group members as catalysts, she was able intuitively to move from turmoil to calm and then to humor. But, in addition to that intuitive trust in her own self-healing mechanism, she also sent out messages through her art about her pain and, later, her joy. Several of Judith's collages, composed of fragmented pieces, illustrated the inner conflict that she was experiencing. That conflict was portrayed in other ways, too, such as being pulled in different directions or buried under rocks.

Judith used the juxtaposed colors of black and red several times in her artwork, an alert to herself and to others about her pain and frustration. In Judith's Conflict Resolution project (Figure 10-3), she tears apart red and black pieces of a painting to create a collage. A streak of red and white penetrates a hole which frames Judith behind a screen door. This image, in addition to the stairways leading up to her in the second pose, might suggest some early sexual trauma to be explored further in her personal therapy sessions.

SECTION THREE
GROUP THERAPY

In attempting to write from a Jungian perspective, we might safely say that group psychotherapy is not one of the strong points of Jungian psychology, primarily because Jung's emphasis was upon the individuation process and development of the personality. Jung, in fact, made strong statements against group psychology. Several of these statements regarding group consciousness appear in his Collected Works. In one such statement, he says, "The group and what belongs to it cover up the lack of genuine individuality, just as parents act as substitutes for everything lacking in their children. In this respect the group exerts a seductive influence, for nothing is easier than a perseveration of infantile ways or a return to them . . . Group observations have confirmed over and over again that the group subtly entices its members into mutual imitation and dependence, thereby holding out the process of sparing them a painful confrontation with themselves" (Collected Works, Vol. 10, pp. 471–472).

Again, in an essay entitled "Techniques of attitude change conducive to world peace," Jung described problems resulting from group behavior, unless group members have completed their individual analysis. He says that "a change of attitude never starts with a group but only with an individual" (Collected Works, Vol. 18, p. 609).

Analyst Thayer Greene (1982) admits that Jung was a skeptic regarding group therapy, but says that Jungians who practice group therapy have found its theoretical formulations in Jung's writings. Greene does not feel that a person should bypass individual for group work, but sees both individual and group treatment as effective adjunctive therapies *after* the analysand has completed some individual analysis.

Another Jungian analyst, James Hall (1977), wrote that Jung believed that group psychotherapy was not a substitute for individual psychoanalysis and that, in group therapy, there is the danger of the client getting stuck on the collective level. Hall suggests that group therapy is a useful container in which to explore some dream images through enactment techniques, although time limitation prevents all members from presenting their dreams. He feels that the interpretative process can be beneficial following enactment of dreams in group therapy, with group members supplying the additional cultural and personal amplification material.

Even though Jung's attitude towards groups and group therapy appeared to be essentially negative, we, like Greene, continue to see the value of the group therapeutic process. From our perspective, groups often provide the energy and enthusiasm needed for personal change. Group members are able to gain access to the personal unconscious, as well as the collective unconscious, and although information gained in this way might be contaminated, as Jung speculated, nevertheless, group members can often gain valuable insights into their own behavior and personality.

Irvin Yalom writes more positively about group psychotherapy. In his book, *The theory and practice of group psychotherapy* (1975), which has become the influential text in the field of group psychotherapy, he divides curative factors in group therapy into eleven primary categories. These categories are: (1) instillation of hope, (2) universality, (3) imparting of information, (4) altruism, (5) the corrective recapitulation of the primary family group, (6) development of socializing techniques, (7) imitative behavior, (8) interpersonal learning, (9) group cohesiveness, (10) catharsis, and (11) existential factors. These factors extend into areas beyond Jung's psychology, but, in recent years, group therapy has become more and more a treatment of choice, both because of its effectiveness in the treatment of clients and its cost effectiveness at a time when mental health treatment costs have skyrocketed.

The use of the expressive arts therapies is also becoming more acceptable and popular in working with groups (Wadeson, Durkin and Perach, 1989). In addition to developing cohesiveness in groups, the expressive arts therapies can be valuable in other instances, such as (1) working with a stuck group, a group which is not doing its work, (2) conflict resolution, helping members on both an individual and group basis to resolve conflicts, (3) identifying feelings, the arts providing a transitional basis or "safety net" for people who are not in touch with feelings, and (4) identifying and reducing individual and group resistances.

With the value of group therapy in mind, we have developed a photo art therapy group method that we call *Visual Transitions*. Visual Transitions is multimodal, using not only photography but movement, art, meditation, video and discussion. The visual transitions method is described in detail in Chapter 11. We have also developed photo art therapy methods to facilitate group cohesion and to deal with stuck or resistant groups. These methods are described in Chapters 12 and 13.

Chapter 11

THE VISUAL TRANSITIONS GROUP

Visual Transitions is a concept that developed from the authors' interest in synthesizing photo and video therapy with art therapy, facilitated within a group setting.

The idea grew from our individual backgrounds in the visual and expressive arts therapies: Corbit in art therapy, movement therapy, and psychodrama; Fryrear in photography, psychodrama, and video.

Our initial plan in developing this method was to combine our two graduate psychology classes and provide an experiential exercise in which the students could experience these therapeutic modalities. The resulting formula has become the basis for various workshops, seminars, group therapy sessions, and presentations initiating personal growth and change.

To achieve its goals, Visual Transitions incorporates still photographs, art, movement, video, and meditation. The participant has the opportunity to observe and experience his or her "stuckness," move to a new, more alive and meaningful state of being, then opt to transit more fully to that state or to determine a comfortable place on the continuum.

Visual Transitions Assignment

The sessions begin with nonverbal introductions. This technique acquaints group members with alternative, visual/kinesthetic means of expressing themselves. Group members sit in a circle. One by one, they introduce themselves nonverbally to the group either from their sitting position or by moving into the circle and relating to group members in their own unique ways. As a rule, this exercise is begun by the group leaders who model their own methods of nonverbal introductions. A few enthusiastic participants have introduced themselves by way of a dance or other movement. This beginning exercise helps to loosen the group and begins to get members in touch with their bodies and used to relying on the visual and kinesthetic senses.

Videotaping can occur throughout the entire session or during any predetermined significant portion. Permission is a necessity before videotaping any therapeutic group activity. Participants want to know what will happen to the videotape and who will see it. If any participants request that they not be videotaped or that any portion of the tape involving them be erased, these requests are honored (see Chapter 14 for more discussion of permission and other ethical considerations).

In the next segment of the session, participants form into pairs to photograph one another. They use instant cameras and take two photographs of each other. One pose describes "As I Was." This pose reflects the participant "As I Was" before therapy, or "As I Was" during a time of emotional conflict, or "As I Was" when entrapped by personal constrictions.

The second pose portrays "As I Would Like to Be." This pose reflects how the client would like to be or to feel ideally.

The poses or postures are often overstated. Someone who had experienced or is experiencing a bout with depression might curl into a fetal position to express this condition nonverbally. Another who was or is afraid might assume a cringing position.

In the second pose, the group member explores and models a body posture which often exaggerates a sense of well-being or change; an open stance with arms lifted to the sky is a common pose.

After the still photos are made, the participants are provided with art materials, including, but not necessarily limited to, poster board, oil pastels, colored chalk, scissors, glue, and colored marking pens.

Each group member then cuts out and mounts the two photographs on poster board in whatever way she wishes, somehow relating the two images to each other with the art materials. When the art projects are completed, members form into pairs or small groups to discuss their work with one another.

Group Processing

After the small groups have discussed their work, they recombine into a large circle. Each member shows his artwork and explains how the two images are related in the art. Immediately after each member's sharing turn, he demonstrates the first pose with his body, then the second. The member is encouraged to repeat the two poses, choosing one word or phrase to describe each pose. The group member concentrates upon the feeling aspect of each pose and the transition movement necessary for moving from one pose to the other. The entire group then joins the presenter in duplicating the movements. Much like the psychodrama technique of mirroring, empathy is developed in assuming the body poses of another person.

The presenter is asked to be aware of personal feelings and body sensations in moving from one pose to the other. Is the pose strained or awkward? Does the presenter feel trapped? Or joyful? The transition is enacted like a group choreography, with members becoming aware not only of their empathic feelings with the presenter, but also attending to personal body sensations and feelings during the reenactment. Each member, therefore, experiences directly the movements described and enacted by themselves and every other group member.

If time permits, the group members might, during this phase, explore their transitions even further by following the transitional action in meditation. One private client who had drawn a rainbow around herself in the "after" pose, took that image into meditation. She visualized herself being surrounded by the rainbow and later described the elated feelings of a natural high which influenced her life in the following weeks.

The videotape of this phase of the therapy program can be replayed immediately after each member's presentation, or at the end of the session or the entire group program. Each member can then see herself going through the transition from "As I Was" to "As I Would Like to Be." Both the art work and the movement become metaphors for change, as do the images captured by the still film and the moving tape.

During one workshop presentation of Visual Transitions, a woman informed us at the end of the workshop that she was angry because we hadn't given her the same opportunity to present her artwork and movements as we had given the other members. We argued that yes, she had presented.

"No," she said, "You passed me by in the group."

When the videotape of her was replayed showing three or four minutes of her presenting her work, she was amazed. "I wouldn't have believed it," she said. The denial mechanism of her personal defense system was far more powerful than she had previously suspected.

The last phase of the program is the general sharing of the experience, relating the experience to more elaborate possible change in the outside world, and sharing common experiences and feelings. It is not unusual for several individuals in a group to demonstrate very similar poses and transitional movements. This similarity is helpful in convincing the group members of the universality of their concerns—a common experience in verbal group therapies also. The last phase is also a time for closure, a time during which members may voice any unspoken issues or feelings.

Discussion

For any therapist, initiating change in clients is a primary concern. Change usually begins with an awareness or insight, but frequently stops there. The client's motivation, ability, or energy resources to move beyond impasse toward change is often lacking in verbal therapy.

Using the expressive means of Visual Transitions, the client gains awareness, experiences the constriction kinesthetically and visually, and uses psychodramatic techniques to move beyond the constriction. Once the impasse is dislodged, the client is then able to experience alternatives in being. Change becomes a choice. Visual records of the new behavior possibilities are available through the still photos and videotaping. How then can the client deny the possibility of change?

Jung (Collected Works, Vol. 16) addressed himself to the idea of being "stuck." He wrote, "In the majority of my cases the resources of the conscious mind are exhausted (or, in ordinary English, they are 'stuck'). It is chiefly this fact that forces me to look for hidden possibilities. For I do not know what to say to the patient when he asks me, 'What do you advise? What shall I do?' I don't know either. I only know one thing: when my conscious mind no longer sees any possible road ahead and consequently gets stuck, my unconscious psyche will react to the unbearable standstill" (pp. 41–42).

We have already discussed the likelihood that the combination of photography, art, and other media will facilitate fantasy and unconscious problem solving. The Visual Transitions method is a particularly good one for facilitating the unconscious in its reaction to the standstill.

Speaking about small changes, Jung had this to say (he was speaking of a dream interpretation): "By such slight changes, which one could never think up rationally, things are set in motion and the dead point is overcome, at least in principle" (Collected Works, Vol. 16, p. 44). The Visual Transitions method is specifically designed to permit, even force, subtle metaphorical or fantasy changes that will set the client in motion and overcome the "dead point." And again, in the same lecture, Jung stated, "Truth to tell, I have no small opinion of fantasy. To me, it is the maternally creative side of the masculine mind. When all is said and done, we can never rise above fantasy. It is true that there are unprofitable, futile, morbid, and unsatisfying fantasies whose sterile nature is immediately recognized by every person endowed with common sense; but the faulty performance proves nothing against the normal performance. All the works of man have their origin in creative imagination. What right, then, have we to disparage fantasy? In the normal course of things, fantasy does not easily go astray; it is too deep for that, and too closely bound up with the taproot of human and animal instinct. It has a surprising way of always coming out right in the end" (pp. 45–46).

Watzlawick, Weakland, and Fisch (1974) suggest implementing small changes in behavior patterns to upset perfectionistic needs and enable one to work toward greater behavior changes. They write that the goal of change is the attempted solution to the problem, and the method chosen for that solution, if it is to be effective, must be translated into the client's language. In Visual Transitions, we are presenting a method in which the client/participant is creating his or her own solution to the problem. The art and body "language" are unique to that person.

Milton Erickson, also, discussed small changes. In his hypnosis therapy Erickson often worked toward altering a client's usual pattern of behavior in some small way, so as to open up the possibility of further change. For example, he would have people who wanted to quit smoking to first alter their smoking pattern by *increasing* the number of cigarettes they were smoking. This alteration in the usual pattern would convince the smoker that change is possible (1980).

Keeney (1983) has also wrestled with the subject of change:

> A lens, or frame of reference, determines the pattern we see, whether it is up or down, distorted or not. A change of lens always invokes a period of initial confusion or transition. If an observer can endure the crisis transition, a new frame will result in an alternative order. The task of epistemological change, although dramatically more difficult, is comparable. Through the lens of cybernetic epistemology, an alternative world will eventually emerge (p. 113).

We have observed dynamic family changes that occur from incidents as seemingly insignificant as directing a child to be put in charge of his bathroom light switch, his first personal responsibility. He has the kinesthetic experience of being in charge of something which directly affects him. The domino effect is soon produced as the child next begins to take control of his own behavior and body functions.

Jean Houston uses body movement to facilitate change in workshop participants. Using imagery, she has group members visualize their bodies achieving greater flexibility and mobility. She then asks them to follow through the visualized movements with body movement. She says that to change behavior, we must change the metaphor: "In our research we have found the metaphors which provide for the personalizing of body arts and states can often give us the charged imagery that then creates those channels of communication for dialogue with our innate body image" (1982, p. 12).

Often in workshops or with individual clients, we will hear the protest, "I can't draw!" Artistic ability is not a prerequisite to the artwork involved in Visual Transitions. During a Visual Transitions presentation to a doctoral entry colloquium, a blind student declined the opportunity to participate in the exercise. She later changed her mind and said she would try even though she had never before attempted an art project. First, she asked a group leader to assist her. She posed for her photographs: the first described how she felt when she entered the graduate program; the second pose described her "as she would like to feel" when she graduated from the program. The leader helped her to cut out her poses. She felt the edges of her photos, then instructed the group leader where she wanted them placed and glued on the poster board. She chose the colors that she wanted and directed the graphics she wanted used with each photograph. The images were impressive. More importantly, she felt that she had scored another victory in overcoming her handicap. She was an artist now.

In a workshop, *Humor in Health Care,* participants were asked to identify a personal constriction, or hang up, which prevented them from living life to its fullest. The Visual Transitions technique was used to help the workshop members to move beyond their constrictions. In the first still photo, workshop participants were asked to model their most binding constriction. Constrictions include such "self-demands" as the need to be perfect, to establish boundaries, to always be in control, to avoid failure (or, conversely, to avoid success), and to please (O'Connell, 1982).

Personal constrictions which hampered life styles of the participants were discussed in small groups. Then members invited others in their groups to help them to find humorous ways in which to change or overcome their constrictions. A second still photo captured the images of the participants overcoming their constrictions in humorous ways. The workshop members discovered that therapy can be fun and that laughing at their own constrictions began to dissipate self-imposed symptoms.

Visual Transitions seems to be a powerful metaphor for change, incorporating still photography, art, meditation, video playback, and group interaction in a single program. As a therapy approach, it can be used either in groups or on an individual basis. Corbit has used the method successfully with children in on-going therapy; and both authors have used it with adults. Children, in fact, who had problems drawing pictures of themselves, found this still photo method to be accurate, exciting and fun.

No particular size of group is more desirable than any other, although obviously size will be restricted by the room area available. Time also creates obvious restrictions. We have found that the ideal time allotment for a session with a group of 14–18 people is approximately three hours. With less time, or more people, the pace is not as leisurely and there is less attention to individuals.

This particular technique is confrontational and should be used with the same caution as any confrontational therapy method. People with fragile diffuse boundaries would need supportive individual therapy prior to or along with any confrontational group therapy including Visual Transitions.

Visual Transitions for Couples

We have introduced a variation of the Visual Transitions group for use with a couple or a group of couples. The couples are usually spouses but could be business partners, lovers, or friends. First, each partner completes the "Who am I in relation to other people?" as described in Chapter 2. They work as partners on the project, helping each other and taking each other's photographs. After that assignment, the couple is asked to pay particular attention to the artwork that depicts the relationship to people of the same gender as the partner. That basic stance toward other men or women forms the background for the relationship to each other. If a man is basically distrustful of women, that basic distrust will form a background for his relationship with his wife. No matter what else, there is always the likelihood that he will be mistrustful of her regardless of her actions.

The next phase is for the couple to show their relationship on a single piece of poster board with photographs of themselves. Their initial impulse may be to pose together for a photograph, but that should be discouraged. It will be more enlightening and productive if, rather than posing together, each partner poses separately. Later, the two photographs can be joined together on the poster board in whatever way the couple can agree upon. The discussion and decision about how to join the photographs is an important step in defining the relationship. Furthermore, the individual photographs emphasize the important fact that the two people are individuals *as well as* a couple, and will always be individuals.

Through discussion and mutual agreement, facilitated by the therapist, the couple decides on the placement of the photographs on the poster board. The placement relative to each other shows the symbolic relationship between the two. With other art materials such as marking pens, ribbon, yarn, construction paper, and so forth the couple can add whatever background and other artifacts they need to depict the relationship.

The therapist should be alert to the dynamics of the relationship during this phase. The dynamics will be revealed in myriad ways. Even something as seemingly simple as choice of color or placement may be highly meaningful to one of the partners. A participant in this assignment related afterward: "Then a very interesting thing happened. No sooner had I put my picture there than Bob immediately started painting around it and closed me off completely. I felt suffocated and alone and rejected in that corner. It was very interesting that I had been very comfortable in that place until I allowed someone else to make me miserable." Typically, the participant did not say anything to her partner at the time. Had the therapist been more alert during the art production, this dynamic of dominance/acquiescence leading to resentment could have been addressed at the time it was happening. Bob was blissfully unaware that he had done anything to cause resentment and could not even remember the incident.

The therapist encourages the partners to continue the assignment until each is satisfied that the work is complete. As each change is made, the partners are instructed to explain and discuss the change with each other. When the couple completes the artwork, they can glue everything down so that it can be handled without displacing the pieces.

The next phase of the Visual Transitions for Couples exercise is for the partners to complete a second poster board, this time depicting their ideal relationship at some time in the future. No doubt the two partners have both similar and different fantasies about where their relationship is headed. This exercise will help them to have a clearer understanding about these similarities and differences and should be helpful in avoiding future disappointments and clashes. The couple proceeds with the art work in much the same way as they did with the previous one, discussing and explaining to each other any additions or changes to the poster board.

With both completed poster boards in front of them, the couple is next instructed to position their bodies in the same pose with the same relationship as in the first poster. They then agree on a label for that pose. Next they pose as in the "ideal" poster and agree on a label for that pose. The couple can then assume the first pose, saying the label out loud, and then the second, saying that label. They are instructed to pay attention to the physical requirements for moving from the "now" pose to the "ideal" pose and to talk about the transition movements. Throughout, the therapist and the couple discuss the "here and now" experience of the movements and draw parallels to the couple's "there and then" real life relationship. Video can be used as with the Visual Transitions Group discussed earlier in this chapter.

Chapter 12

DEVELOPMENT OF GROUP COHESION

How does a group become cohesive? What happens within a group to cause individual members to begin to feel a part of a group and to begin to identify with other group members? What transforms a group of strangers into a community of trusting individuals, persons who can disclose secrets, possibly never before told, persons who can support and encourage others in their struggles with life problems?

The authors, over a period of the last ten years or more, have watched this process occur spontaneously in photo art therapy seminars and workshops. For the past several years, we have led groups with the objective of facilitating and observing this group cohesion process.

From our experience, this bonding occurs at different time periods depending upon group members and the group experience, but it appears to happen more quickly when the arts are used. The expressive arts therapies seem to facilitate and intensify this group cohesion experience, possibly because of the addition of the nonverbal medium of communication, which is not available in most process groups, or because members become less constricted as they interact through movement, phototherapy, and the arts. Even through the eyes of trained observers and group members with years of clinical experience, this process of group bonding is quickened through the arts.

What is the value of having members of a group develop a feeling of cohesion? Don't they then lose their individuality? Many persons have never experienced a sense of belonging: an objective that brings many individuals into therapy, and especially into group psychotherapy. This feeling of cohesion or belonging is ordinarily developed at an early age within one's own family or in early relationships. But if that stage of development is bypassed or not experienced, then the individual remains needy for that feeling of connection. In individual therapy, the transference phenomenon creates or recreates that connection necessary for healing, but the bonding can also occur when a person comes into group therapy. Often, group members who have never experienced intimacy get a "high" when group bonding occurs.

The photo art therapy model that we have developed to promote cohesion in groups is as follows:

(1) *Introductions.* When strangers come together to form a group, it is first necessary to get a sense of their individuality. This can begin to happen by asking group members what they wish to get out of the workshop or group.

(2) *Divide into subgroups.* This process is especially important if the workshop is large. When there are more than eight people in a workshop, then smaller groups are formed. This can be done spontaneously through self-selection, or through a "count off" method, where groups are formed from every other person or every third person.

(3) *Decide on a theme for poster.* Working within the small group context, members decide on a theme for their first poster. This process might take a short period of time, or, for some groups, it can be a slow, deliberate process.

(4) *Photography.* Members of the subgroup decide upon and discuss their poses, then select a site to do their photography. If the weather is pleasant and conditions right, they might even choose to go out-of-doors for this part of the project. In some groups, members help and encourage one another with their poses.

(5) *Assignment of personal space on poster.* When the group reassembles around their poster, they then select a place on the poster board for their photographic image. The images are not glued down at this time, because group interactions can easily cause the placement to change.

(6) *Artwork.* Group members next consider the artwork for their poster, both in regards to decorating around their personal image and in the context of the theme of the group poster. Oil pastels, colored marking pens, chalks, art tissue, ribbon, and yarn can be used for the artwork.

(7) *Glue down images.* When members are satisfied with their image placement and the overall artwork, they can then glue down their images.

(8) *Group process.* Members process their experience with their group and group leader or leaders.

(9) *Psychodrama.* The group at this time might consider doing a psychodrama, taking either an aspect of the poster to dramatize or the entire poster.

(10) *Follow-up poster.* A follow-up poster or posters can provide fur-

ther development of the group as members interact both through their images and in person.

In mid-January of 1991, we began a short-term, experiential group to enable us to gather illustrations for this chapter. The group consisted of eight persons: seven women and one man. Three of the group members were graduate psychology students, two of the members were mental health workers; all were interested in self-growth, social interaction, and the opportunity to experience the expressive arts therapies. All agreed that the group artwork could be published. The following are descriptions of the sessions in which we paid particular attention to the process of developing group cohesiveness:

Session #1, January 15, 1991

The first group session began late. Only eight of the eleven persons who had signed up for the group experience arrived at 1:00 p.m., the assigned starting time. We gave the additional three persons several minutes to locate the building and clinic, then began without them.

The group room was small, with a sofa and chairs. A two-way mirror normally used for student teaching was on one wall of the group room. We would not be using the mirror for our group. Introductions began with names, and a short explanation of why members wanted to participate in this experiential group.

As group leaders, we began by explaining to the group-as-a-whole the purpose for the sessions: primarily to look at the process of developing cohesiveness in the group setting, to collect data for this chapter, and to provide a group experience for those interested in the process. We wanted group members to attend all sessions, if possible, and expected them to call if, for some reason, they were not able to attend a session.

In explaining the photo art therapy process, we told the group members that they would form into pairs to photograph one another. The still photos were to express how participants felt at the moment as members of this new group. They were then to position the photos onto a community poster board, trimming the photos or not, as they so choose. Rather than to interact totally in person, the group members now had the option to also interact through their photos on the poster board. The photos could be moved into different positions until all members were satisfied with their places on the poster. Next, art materials (oil pastels, colored markers, art tissue, construction paper, and yarn) were made available to group members, so that they could embellish the poster in any creative manner they saw fit.

After we, as leaders, gave instructions, the members photographed one another. Most of the participants appeared to be somewhat tense during their posing, which is to be expected in a beginning group. In workshops, this tension can, as a rule, be reduced by having group members introduce themselves nonverbally. These nonverbal introductions take many forms from simply walking around the circle and making eye contact with other participants, to an introduction by an occasional "free spirit," which might take the form of a somersault or a dance step or other creative personal expression of oneself.

After all of the photographs were completed, the group members sat around the poster board on the floor. For this first poster, the group members apparently misinterpreted our instructions. Rather than placing their photo onto the poster and decorating around the photo, they, instead, individually did art work around their photos before placing the photos onto the poster (this "misinterpretation" may have been a way for the group members to avoid premature close encounters).

Selecting one's space on the poster is an important part of the process. Does one select the center? A corner? The top? The bottom? In our group, four of the members immediately selected the corners for their space. Liz, one of the group members, was cautious about entering into the group process, taking a long time to complete her yellow, stick-like appendages that radiated from around her photo.

Margie's photo had yellow and orange tissue paper strips coming from around her photo. She placed her photo near the bottom edge of the poster board. When she talked about the placement, she said that she might like to be in the center. But, after trying the center space briefly, she abandoned it, saying that it did not feel comfortable.

Laurie added yellow yarn to her photo and eventually made contact with others by stringing her yarn to their photos.

Dan was seated in his photo. There was a black area at the bottom of his artwork. Group members speculated that the black area might be a pedestal or an African cooking pot.

As the group members talked, they began to move their photo images closer together. Laurie remained cautious, and stayed somewhat outside the circle of group members on the poster. Some of the participants talked about not wanting to glue their photos down, but as time grew to a close, they positioned and glued the photos onto the poster.

Margie finally positioned herself in the center of the poster, reaching out to the other members. Members observed that all photos had some sort of barriers around them—simultaneously reaching out, yet protecting themselves. Anna kept herself protected inside of a bottle drawn around her photo. She said that she might sometime in the future come out of the bottle, that she might become more outgoing.

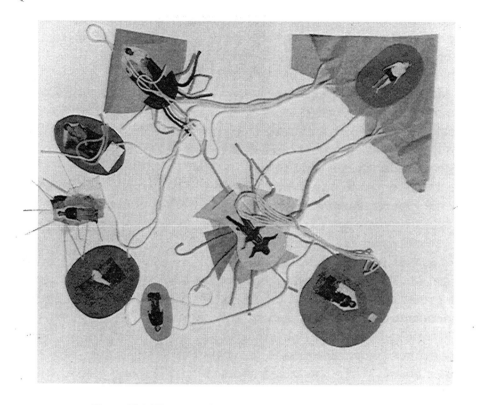

Figure 12-1. The group begins. Separate but connected.

The issue of Masonic symbols and the secrecy of the organization were discussed toward the end of the group session. We might speculate that this discussion was the group's way of communicating to one another and to the leaders about confidentiality and secrecy regarding personal material brought up during the sessions. It could also be the group members' way of describing their desire to be a part of a secret or mystery group.

Session #2, January 29, 1991

Seven members showed up for the group today. Fryrear placed last week's poster onto the middle of the floor, and said that for today's poster members would be expected to move their images only a bit.

The group members looked at the poster from their chairs in silence for some time. Jennifer said that she had become confused about the instructions last week. She thought that we had said to place the images onto the poster before doing the art work.

Corbit said, "Yes, those were the instructions, but the group's interpretation is the most important factor."

After more hesitation on the group member's parts, Fryrear set the cameras out for them. Still, the group did not move towards doing its work.

Margie finally decided how she wanted to be photographed, and urged the rest of the group to begin their photos.

As members began to work on the poster, they seemed more insulated or protective of themselves than during the last session. As they began to place their photos onto the poster, the theme of "hands" emerged. The hands provided both a protective barrier and a symbol of reaching out to one another.

Jan said that she would be absent the next week because her daughter would be having a baby. Someone suggested that she be photographed ahead of time so that she could be added to the group project the following week. Jan agreed, and posed holding a "baby" (made of paper and tissue).

Session #3, February 5, 1991

Today's group began with the members viewing the previous two posters. Dan and Liz had not processed their work from the previous week, and took time to discuss their parts of the poster. Dan seemed unsure about his work, which was comprised of two large hands holding two phases of himself, "like a crystal ball."

Liz's image was arranged over a yellow background with pieces of purple confetti at the top. Her association to her work was that of not being totally a part of the group.

Margie suggested a tree theme for Poster #3. Others asked what kind of tree, but she offered no specific suggestion. The group members all agreed to the theme of a tree. She cut out the trunk, then attempted

Figure 12-2. The group reaching out to each other.

positions for it on the poster, beginning low on the page, then raising it to the middle. The group members agreed that roots would be important in the poster. We heard light-hearted comments this week, such as, "Shall we swing on vines or be monkeys?" Taking the initiative, Margie was obviously, at this point, emerging as the group's leader.

Linda mentioned that she wasn't sure if she was being "real" in the group, or if she was "real" outside of the group. She sensed a difference in these two personas, or aspects, of herself.

Laurie seemed to be more active during this session. Her contribution to the poster included using wet tissue paper to color the sky and the ground.

Jan's photo from the previous week, holding an "infant," was glued onto a yellow sun by Linda and placed into the top left-hand corner. In her absence, "She was distant from the group," someone said.

Anna remained remote from the group during the entire session. She said that she was feeling claustrophobic in the small warm room and, in fact, she left the room at one point to get air. We discussed leaving the door open for more air circulation. Anna placed her work in the bottom left-hand corner where she pictured herself hanging from a vine on a dead-looking tree. Dan talked about flying or leaping off a tree limb. Margie said that she would catch him. She was offering him the security for which he seemed to be asking. Protective barriers appeared to be coming down in the group.

Linda worked independently during this session as she cut tree leaves out of tissue paper. She finally added the leaves to the poster, symbolically joining the group.

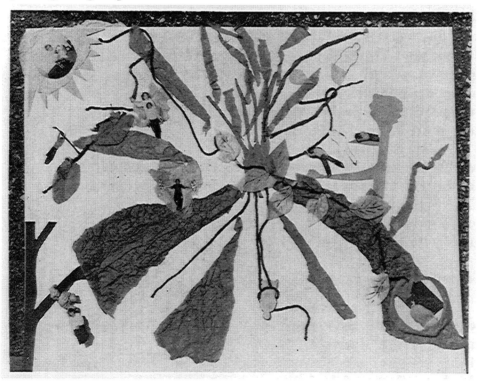

Figure 12-3. A common theme, "The Tree."

Our time was up before the group processed their tree. There was talk about five weeks not being enough time, could the group continue? The sessions were half over and the members felt they wouldn't have enough time to do their work.

Session #4, February 12, 1991

Liz was absent from today's session. We began the group by viewing last week's poster of the tree, reacquainting members with the group interaction on the poster. The group members gained new perspectives into their group's development as they talked about where they had been at the beginning of the group's formation, and where they are now.

We suggested a theme for the fourth group session, "The Group Dream." We wanted to offer the group members freedom within a structure, so, for members to create a dream would give them the opportunity to fantasize openly about the group. The group started with a round-robin story, with each member adding to or embellishing the fantasy.

As the members began to discuss and to recreate the dreamstory in various segments, the poster took on a holiday spirit. In one segment the group was at a fair, riding on a carousel. The group members rode on animals, which the members contributed to the poster. In a second segment of the fantasy, the group members were engrossed in a conversation while sitting around a table.

In a fourth part of the dream, a boat was added. Jan came late to the session, she "had almost forgotten about the group session." After studying the poster for several minutes, Jan added herself to the boat segment. Others were invited to join in the boat scene, but declined. Then the group members stated that they were testing how they felt in different parts of the poster.

Session #5, February 19, 1991

The group began by focusing on Liz who was absent the previous week. Liz seemed unsure as to how she could fit into the group "dream" fantasy. Finally, Margie volunteered to photograph Liz. Liz posed in a sitting position, then cut out a blue cloud and placed herself on the cloud near the top of the poster.

The group next decided to put themselves around a camp fire. They all seemed pleased with this segment of the dream poster.

Next, Linda photographed the two leaders, cut out the photos in circles, and placed them into the cave. Other group members commented that the photos looked like two eyes peering out of the cave. "Two wise eyes," one of the group members commented. The "two wise eyes" can be viewed as the group's projection on the leaders, who remained fairly unobtrusive during the making of the posters.

There was light-hearted joking with one another during the second half of the group session. Group members discussed their "hope anchor," which they felt needed color or glitter.

Margie said she'd like to "get on with" the next poster. Fryrear responded that he felt the group possibly had more work to complete on this one.

Anna suggested that the group members photograph one another and arrange their images in a circular, or a mandala shape. The group discussed whether they should be placed head or feet towards the center. They decided to pose with arms outstretched, touching one another. When they placed their photos onto the poster, the pictures formed a circle. Some of their comments included, they "looked like a sky-diving team," and they "looked like a ferris wheel."

Linda glued on a package that she had made and group members talked about what they would like their gift to be. Linda mentioned she would like some popcorn, a diet coke, some Mozart, and a good novel. Margie dittoed the remarks, but changed it to some non-alcoholic wine.

The group members next lined up all four posters to compare them. The first, they remarked, was protected; the second, they began to reach out with symbolic hands; in the third, they used a tree theme; and the fourth portrayed the group's fantasy dream.

By the end of the session, the group members were not ready for closure. Again, they suggested more sessions, or an ongoing group. They discussed how close they felt to one another. They had, in fact, met together for lunch before this fifth session. Liz suggested that they gather names and addresses so that they could keep in touch with one another. Most time-limited therapy groups resist the termination process, that time of saying goodbye, and attempt to find ways to continue the group.

In reviewing the group development, we paid particular attention to the resistances, and the dropping of resistances, both at the beginning and throughout the length of the sessions. What did the group members' photographic body language say about defending themselves against the group? What about the protective shields group members placed around their images, through "misinterpretation" of the instructions in their first posters?

We looked at other factors in the group process, such as who assumed the leadership role in the group. We have observed in the past that when groups are composed mostly of women, with one or two men, it is common for a man to assume or be "nudged" into the leadership role. Dan, apparently, chose not to take on that role. Margie, for the most part,

Figure 12-4. The fourth and last group poster, incorporating a "mandala" of all of the members in the center.

assumed the role of leader. Linda, too, in her own quiet way, was influential in the group.

In our final summary, did the group meet our expectations of developing cohesion? In all, the group with its hour and a half per week time schedule spent approximately seven and a half hours together. During that period, the group went from, on the whole, very defended persons to members who had developed into a cohesive group. A sense of trust developed as they shared intimacies, exchanged names and addresses, found ways to spend more time together, and even requested a continuation of the group sessions. We felt that these eight individuals had come a long way in developing a sense of group cohesion from the time they first met together in mid-January.

Chapter 13

THE STUCK GROUP

One of the nightmares of group therapists is having a group that is "stuck," a group that remains bogged down in their work to a point where nothing therapeutic is happening. Some of the symptoms of the stuck group include: (1) the group becomes dominated by one or two members, (2) members might be stuck on one irrelevant or tangential topic, (3) no one says anything, (4) members begin coming late or don't come at all, (5) members begin looking at their watches or looking bored, (6) subgrouping begins, or (7) group members start complaining.

What does a group therapist do when these symptoms begin to occur? The therapist might first begin to explore her own personal attitude towards the group, and, of course, look at what is going on in the lives of individual group members as contributing factors to the group's apathy.

The leader must, first of all, have well-thought-out therapeutic goals for the group, which act as preventative measures for group constriction and help to facilitate solutions, if and when constriction does occur. These goals can include, but are not limited to: developing group cohesion, ventilation of feelings, a blueprint for unsticking the stuck group, and facilitating communication between group members.

As group leader, one of your first actions in unsticking that stuck group is to get rid of the chairs. Sitting in a circle and talking obviously isn't working for the group at this time. So, if you're stuck in that format, find a different format to begin to change the structure.

As a start, for a format change, you might solicit suggestions from your group members. You might ask, for example, how complaints can be redirected into a more positive framework, or, how members have experienced becoming unstuck in their personal lives in the past. With no group suggestions, the leader might propose one of the expressive arts therapies, such as psychodrama, clay sculpting, painting, or phototherapy. Dream work can also provide a format change, or, possibly, the reading and processing of a fairy tale or some poetry.

Using photo art therapy as an example, this medium can begin to give group members a new vantage point for both the group interactions and for where they are on a personal level. If unresolved conflicts between group members are causing the apathetic climate, then the photo art therapy can become a safe and effective way in which to encounter another member or members. Or, on the other hand, one member might have difficulty in expressing his sexual attraction, or feelings of closeness, for another member. Interaction on the poster between still photos can sometimes speak louder than words.

A photo art therapy experience can provide boundaries in an open-ended group. The structure built into this exercise includes time and space limitations, art supplies, and the poster board (which becomes a metaphor for the group boundaries). The structure provides safety and guarantees interaction between group members as they form photographic dyads, and, later, relate to one another through their art creations. Putting the group on paper involves all members of the group, even those who might prefer to isolate themselves. Any creative expression of self-imposed isolation also becomes a part of the group process.

In this photo art therapy exercise, the group leader assumes the role of facilitator providing additional structure through his guidance to get started, allowing interaction and creativity of group members. The leader remains as unobtrusive as possible, which, in turn, permits the group to do their work.

As the group art creation takes shape on the poster board, group members can move their photos around on the poster until they feel satisfied with their place in the group. For this reason glue is not provided until the group processes its original poster. The glue represents commitment, or, on the other hand, it can also be a metaphor for being stuck. When group members are totally satisfied with their poster, they can glue down the images and do a final processing of the work. It is during this final processing that the group leader can again play a more active role, that is, unless the group members are vigorously processing their own work.

In presenting this work to groups of mental health professionals, we ask that participants consider a time when they, themselves, felt the discomfort of leading a stuck group, or they might simply imagine that they are members of a stuck group. As a warm-up exercise, the group members are asked to assume poses that identify their stuck positions. A pose might be enacted by a participant lying prone on the floor as an incompetent group leader, helpless to deal with the group members' or his own passivity. Another group member might assume a pose of being stuck to a chair, with feet stuck to the floor and hands stuck together—totally passive, totally defenseless.

As the group members find their poses, other members of the group photograph them, capturing kinesthetically and visually their sense of inadequacy. As the group members work on their poster together, they are able to empathize with one another in their feelings of helplessness.

The second poster begins with some "shaking loose" exercises, or, possibly, some upbeat music, which helps to loosen the constricted feelings of being stuck. Group members might tap their feet or even dance to the music. Not surprisingly, participants become almost buoyant as they work on their second poses and the artwork surrounding their pictures. Although both the constricted and the "getting unstuck" poses are simulated, nevertheless, group members respond dramatically to the freedom represented in their unconstricted poses, their artwork, and their communal creativity.

Resistance in groups

One of the more common problems that therapists face when leading groups, and a likely cause of a group being stuck, is that of client/patient resistance. The resistance can take the form of withdrawal, or it can be active resistance whereby the client/patient is overtly antagonistic towards the group leader or other group members. A photo art therapy method that we have developed to identify and to overcome resistance is to have the group members purposely act out and verbalize their resistances to being in the group.

At the beginning of the group session, members consider reasons why they would rather not be in the group. The reasons can be actual or, if they choose, they can make up a reason. Next, group members translate their resistance into body language and introduce themselves to the group, first using their body language poses and next verbalizing to other group members why they don't want to be a participant. This becomes an educational model for therapy group members to learn to verbalize problems rather than to "act out."

In the next step, the group is asked to devise a group body sculpture in which all members participate, demonstrating their "resistance" poses. The group sculpture can then be photographed by one of the leaders. This photograph can later become a part of the group poster.

Group members then select a photography partner. Dividing into partners can be reassuring when faced with the prospect of relating to an entire group of people. The most common procedure would be to choose the person sitting next to you. Our favorite method in working with large workshop groups is to encourage a simple "milling" process whereby participants move slowly around the room until they "find" a partner. If there are an uneven number of individuals, one group can be composed of three partners.

The photography partners first discuss their poses for their poster, then photograph one another. This activity forces additional communication between partners as they consider their poses, select the site for the photography, and interact through the photo process.

When the photography is completed, the partners gather with their small group (usually six to eight members) around their poster board. Group members next interact on the poster, using their photo images and other art materials to embellish or decorate the poster. It is best if members wait until the poster art is finished to glue down their images.

In one workshop that we led, a woman participant came in very angry. As it happened, our room assignment had been changed several times, to the dismay of everyone involved. This woman had waited for elevators, had been up and down in the building, and had been sent to several rooms before she found us. Her anger became her resistance. During her group's work, she was able to see how powerful and frightening her anger was to those around her. As she attempted to reach out to others symbolically through her art, they withdrew because of their fear of her explosive nature. The poster became a healthy arena in which she could explore and to begin to resolve the depths of her anger.

Although this method can be useful in many different types of groups, it can be especially helpful to group leaders when they are working with a "captive" group: a hospital group in which the treatment program insists upon patients' attendance in groups, a prison group, a perpetrators' group, etc. In addressing the members' resistances at the onset, that oppositional attitude or behavior is defused and can become a part of the group process. These resistances are discussed, they are felt kinesthetically, they are viewed through the photographic images, and they are put into a group art creation.

Looking at the many methods of learning, this procedure self-educates by activating our senses of seeing, hearing, touching. This learning about oneself, therefore, takes place on many different levels and becomes integrated learning. In addition, the learning is seldom painful, as is often the case in confrontational groups, but is usually fun and enjoyable.

SECTION FOUR
DISCUSSION

In this last short section, we discuss the problem of confidentiality, the practical matter of materials, some other methods of photo art therapy that we have not covered elsewhere in the book, discernable trends, and a summary of the book.

Because the facial features of clients may be recognizable in a photograph, confidentiality takes on a new dimension with photo art therapy. It is not enough to disguise personal information about clients, their photographs must be protected in some way also. There is also the interesting problem of ownership. Who owns the photo, the camera operator or the person in the photograph?

For the beginning photo art therapist, we give a basic list of materials that would be necessary for a photo art therapy program.

There are several interesting photo art therapy programs that are not generally well known. Many artists and photographers who are using photographs therapeutically would much rather make art and do therapy than write articles. Programs we happen to know about and that are primarily photo art therapy are included in Chapter 14.

Chapter 15 is a brief summary of the book.

Chapter 14

ETHICAL AND PRACTICAL CONSIDERATIONS

The Problem of Confidentiality

Mental health professionals, by training and perhaps by inclination, are sensitive to confidentiality and other ethical issues. The American Psychological Association and the American Art Therapy Association have codes of ethics, and a confidentiality clause is prominent is each. The American Psychological Association confidentiality principle reads:

> Psychologists have a primary obligation to respect the confidentiality of information obtained from persons in the course of their work as psychologists. They reveal such information to others only with the consent of the person or the person's legal representative, except in those unusual circumstances in which not to do so would result in clear danger to the person or to others. Where appropriate, psychologists inform their clients of the legal limits of confidentiality.
>
> a. Information obtained in clinical or consulting relationships, or evaluative data concerning children, students, employees, and others, is discussed only for professional purposes and only with persons clearly concerned with the case. Written and oral reports present only data germane to the purposes of the evaluation, and every effort is made to avoid undue invasion of privacy.
>
> b. Psychologists who present personal information obtained during the course of professional work in writings, lectures, or other public forums either obtain adequate prior consent to do so or adequately disguise all identifying information.
>
> c. Psychologists make provisions for maintaining confidentiality in the storage and disposal of records.
>
> d. When working with minors or other persons who are unable to give voluntary, informed consent, psychologists take special care to protect these persons' best interests (American Psychological Association Ethics Committee, 1990, pp. 390–395).

The American Art Therapy Association Confidentiality Principle reads:

> Art therapists have a primary responsibility to respect client confidentiality and safeguard verbal and visual information about an individual or family that has been obtained in the course of their practice, investigation or teaching.

A. Information shall be revealed only to professionals concerned with the case. Written and oral reports only disclose data relevant to the purposes of the inquiry. Every effort is made to avoid undue invasion of privacy.

B. Art therapists are responsible for informing their clients of the limits of confidentiality.

C. Art therapists obtain written permission from clients involved before any data, visual or verbal, is divulged. All identifying information about the individual is adequately disguised.

D. Art therapists may reveal information without the consent of their clients when there is clear and immediate danger to an individual or to society, or as mandated by law. Such information is revealed only to appropriate professional workers, public authorities or others designated by law.

E. Art therapists make provisions for maintaining confidentiality in storage and disposal of records. (American Art Therapy Association Ethics Committee, 1988, pp. 15–16.)

In addition to confidentiality issues, both organizations address other ethical considerations such as professional relations and welfare of clients. The American Art Therapy Association adds a section on public use and reproduction of client art. We urge all readers who are not familiar with these codes to read them in detail.

Photography and video, because of the captured facial features of clients, raise the possibility of a breach of confidence. It is not enough to simply guard against revealing background information that may allow clients to be identified. The image itself may be recognized by other people. For that reason, special steps need to be taken before using cameras in therapy.

Clients, first and foremost, want to know what is going to happen to the photograph or videotape and who is going to see it. We make it a point to discuss with clients the exact disposition of the photograph or tape. If the therapist is under supervision, and a supervisor is to view the photograph or tape, the client must know that and agree to it. Usually, it is best to allow the client to keep the artwork containing the photographs or to keep the videotape, so that there is no possibility of anyone seeing them without the client's permission. That procedure is possible in individual therapy. Unfortunately, in group work, there may be other group members on the tape or possibly in the photograph. In those cases, it is best for the therapist to safeguard the work, or to erase or destroy it, with a clear understanding among the group members as to the disposition of the work. In cases where the work is to be used for educational purposes, such as in this book, it is necessary to obtain written permission from each person whose image is shown before the work can be published. The client may ask that the image be disguised in some way.

Some mental health facilities have explicit policies regarding the taking of photographs on the premises. One art therapist in Houston was prevented from using photographs in therapy because the hospital had a policy against taking *any* photographs of patients. In such a case it might be possible to get permission from the ward supervisor or hospital administration before beginning the project, if the project is explained fully. Most people assume that photography simply means taking snapshots of patients, and administrators might have the idea that the photographs will be shown to the general public. If it is explained that clients will keep the photographs, and that no other patients will be included in the photos, then the confidentiality fears will be greatly reduced. In most of the projects discussed in this book, the images are strictly individual with no group poses. In any event, it is sound policy to discuss the use of photographs or video with the mental health administration, as well as the participants, *prior* to implementing such a program.

Weiser (1986) has written a thoughtful essay on the ethics of photographs in therapy. One issue she raises is the ownership of the photo or negative. If the therapist owns the film and camera and takes a photograph of a client, who owns the image, the therapist or client? Or, to complicate matters, if the mental health agency owns the camera and film, and the therapist works for the agency, then who owns the photograph? These details must be discussed and resolved with the client, and the agency administration, before using cameras in therapy.

Some clients do not want to be photographed or videotaped. Those wishes should be honored. In an art therapy program, a client can always draw himself in lieu of a photograph, or can watch and not actively participate in part of the therapy. A client who does not want to be in front of a camera may be included in the project behind the camera, by appointing him the camera operator.

Safety does not seem to be a concern with the projects we have discussed in this book, but there is one safety topic that needs to be addressed. The instant film has two layers of paper with the developing chemicals sandwiched between. When the image is cut out, the seal holding the chemicals is broken and a minute amount of development chemicals is released. Sometimes there is a slight tingling sensation on the fingers. The Polaroid Corporation cautions against cutting the film, but in some ten years of using the Polaroid film and cutting out the images, we have not had any problems. We advise participants to wash their hands after handling the cut-out prints, and to avoid putting the prints, or their fingers, on the eyes or mouth. The latter admonition would be most relevant to young children or individuals with severe mental handicaps. In these cases, it is unlikely and inadvisable that the participants would be cutting the images apart anyway.

Art Materials

We have been pleased with the Polaroid 600 cameras. They are easy to use and very sturdy. We have used them on the beach, in the woods, with young children, and under other adverse conditions, with few problems. The pictures are in color and are clear. The added benefit of being able to see the developed photo just one minute after exposure is of paramount importance. A simple camera with built-in flash costs about $30.00 and a somewhat more sophisticated one about $45.00. We have been able to buy twin packs of film (20 exposures) on sale for $15.00–$18.00. If these amounts of money are prohibitive, do not overlook the possibility of support from service organizations. The Rotary Club has donated film for projects, and other service organizations will likely be receptive to requests for help. One nonprofit mental health center in Houston succeeded in obtaining cameras and film donated directly from the Polaroid Corporation.

White or colored poster board makes a good background for most art projects. We often cut the poster board in two, so that it will last twice as long and so that the client is not confronted with so large a space to fill with art. For large group projects, mural paper or drawing paper is useful for a background.

The therapist can use almost any art materials to add to the photographs. We like to use colored marking pens, oil pastels, construction paper and tissue paper, and colored yarn. Many therapists will want to use acrylic or water-based paints and brushes. Glue sticks, art paste and liquid glue are necessary also. There is one technical problem with the use of colored construction paper or tissue paper and the photographs. When a photograph is glued on top of colored paper, liquid glue will cause the color to bleed through the photograph. That can be prevented by using a glue stick, in moderation, to adhere the photographs to colored paper.

As a quick and easy guide, here is a list of supplies that a beginning photo art therapist should acquire:

Polaroid 600 camera and film
White poster board
Assorted colors of poster board, including black.
Colored marking pens
Oil pastels
Assorted colors of tissue paper, including black and white
Assorted colors of construction paper, including black and white
Small boxes. Packaging stores sell boxes in several sizes. We like ones that are approximately 8″ square. Shoe boxes or other small boxes are suitable as well.
Assorted colors of yarn, including black and white
Assorted colors of ribbons, including black and white
Scissors
Glue sticks
Liquid glue
Art paste
Glitter, spangles, and colored feathers
Aluminum foil
Several old magazines with lots of pictures

Trends and Other Possible Applications

In this book we have not, by any means, exhausted the possibilities of using photographs in art therapy. We, ourselves, have developed or at least tried many other programs, and other people have as well. At one point Fryrear and Krauss (1983) identified eleven broad areas in which photographs are used therapeutically. The eleven areas are (1) the evocation of emotional states, (2) the elicitation of verbal behavior, (3) modeling, (4) mastery of a skill, (5) facilitation of socialization, (6) creativity/ expression, (7) diagnostic adjunct to verbal therapies, (8) a form of nonverbal communication between client and therapist, (9) documentation of change, (10) prolongation of certain experiences, and (11) self-confrontation. If we include video in our discussion of photo art therapy the list grows even longer. In the present book, we have concentrated on the use of photographs in creative/expressive ways in combination with other art media.

There is no doubt that art therapy is enjoying a burst of popularity as a treatment modality. In just the last few years, art therapists have been recognized as distinctly qualified professionals with their own certification standards. The incorporation of photo and video into art therapy is, of course, a much smaller and more specialized endeavor, but that specialization, too, seems to be growing in sophistication and popularity.

The American Art Therapy Association routinely has one or more sessions on photography or video in their annual national conference program.

Without going into great detail, we would like to mention in this chapter several other approaches that are in the beginning stages or that do not fit neatly into the format of this book as complete chapters.

One great need for innovative therapeutic approaches is in the area of child abuse. The children who are being abused, the adults who are abusing the children, and adults who were abused as children are all in need of help. Adult survivors of abuse, like Judith in Chapter 10, have received most of the attention. Abusing adults are likely to be the focus of attention of legal or protective authorities, tangential to the children, who are being protected. The children themselves are frequently placed in group homes or foster homes by Children's Protective Services.

The children who are placed in foster homes or other homes away from their families may be protected from the abusing family member, but they often feel victimized by the placement as well. They are taken away from their friends, their school, their pets, sometimes their siblings and other relatives. They feel punished by their protection. The children also feel that they are somehow to blame for their plight, and often feel angry and misunderstood as well. They are apprehensive about the future and may feel alienated and alone. They suffer from low self-esteem and lack confidence and the ability to see their own strengths.

Fryrear and Price (1991) have developed an art therapy program to help ease the transition of children into protective care. The program is seven weeks in length, one and one-half to two hours each week, and includes photography and video as well as drawing, painting, and discussion. The program has as its immediate goals (1) letting the children tell their stories, (2) helping the children gain perspective on the current protective situation, (3) helping the children realize that they are not at fault, (4) helping the children see that they have a support group, and (5) helping the children see their own strengths. A general goal is to help insure that the foster placement will be a successful one. A long-term goal, along with the entire protective care system, is to break the cycle of abuse that is handed down from generation to generation. The program is designed for children ages six to sixteen, and is conducted in small groups of five or six children. A brief outline of the program follows:

Session 1. "This Is My Story." The children compose a poster about their current predicament, coming into protective care, and tell the group about it. Included in the picture is a Polaroid photograph of themselves, posed whichever way they want, augmented with colored marking pens.

Session 2: "It Didn't Happen Overnight." On a poster board, the children draw three bad things that have happened to them, and tell the group about it.

Session 3: "It's Not My Fault." Using the poster board from Session 2, the children write one statement about each of the three events. They are then videotaped, in a talk show format with the group leader as the talk show host, showing the art work and reading the statements. The "host" interjects with the remark that it is the adult who was supposed to control himself, and the statement, "It's not your fault" after each reading. The entire group responds with a chorus of "It's not my fault." In a recent group, we changed the format from a talk show to a musical number, with the statements that the children wrote becoming the lyrics to a musical number with the refrain, "It's not my fault, I'm not to blame." The children were enthusiastic about that program.

Session 4: "It's Not All Bad." On a poster board, children draw three good things that have happened to them, and tell the group about the poster.

Session 5: "I'm Not Alone." On a sheet of paper with silhouettes of people on it, each child pastes a photograph of herself in the middle and then draws in faces and names of people who are supportive. Schoolmates, relatives, teachers, group leaders, and foster parents are some possible supporters.

Session 6: "I've Got What It Takes." Each child constructs a coat of arms on a precut poster board, including strengths and a positive motto.

Session 7: The children and all of their foster parents meet together and the children show the foster parents all of their work from the past six sessions.

To date (September, 1991) Price has conducted two groups using the program and we are beginning a third one with a different therapist. The group experience seems to be very helpful to the children.

Powell and Faherty (1990) report on a 20-week art therapy program for the treatment of sexually-abused children. They did not include photography, but they did have several sessions using video, including the playing of educational tapes and making of videotaped dramas by the group members.

Jacobs (1991) works with sexually-abused adolescent girls by enlarging self-portrait Polaroid photographs 200 times with a copy machine. The enlarged images are glued onto cardboard backing and a base stand is added. The girls make two additional cardboard images, the perpetrator and the protector. Photographs of men cut from magazines are used for the perpetrator and the girls' own images are used for the protector. The girls dress the images in paper clothing cut from magazines and dramas are played out and discussed around the triangle of victim, perpetrator, and protector.

A video art therapy program has been developed and tested by Fryrear and Stephens (1988, 1990). In this program, the video becomes an integral part of the therapy, rather than an adjunct to it. Video has been used a great deal in therapy, as we mentioned in the Introduction, but rarely as a component in an art therapy program.

Clients are provided with art materials, such as poster board, colored construction paper, tissue paper, marking pens, feathers, glitter, colored yarn, scissors, and glue. They are then instructed to make a mask. Masks, although frequently used to express one's persona, also reveal one's private or unconscious fantasies. The ambiguous task of constructing a mask results in a projection of the mask maker's personality, similar to telling a story in response to a Thematic Apperception Test plate or reacting to a Rorschach ink blot. An assumption, borne out by research, is that clients project into the mask a part of the personality that is not well-integrated, or perhaps not accepted or even denied.

After the mask is completed, the clients put on their masks, or hold them in front of their faces, and look into a video camera. Using cue cards, the clients utter a series of prescribed statements or questions. Later, the clients, without the masks, view the video playback of the masked persona and respond to the statements or questions. The result is a dialogue between the client and the facet of personality that is represented symbolically by the mask. The goal of the dialogue is the integration of the projected personality part represented by the mask, and the rest of the personality. In Jung's theoretical framework, the clients are trying to individuate, or to integrate these unconscious or denied projections.

The series of statements or questions written on the cue cards are designed to facilitate integration or individuation, in a graduated way, from awareness, through acceptance, to integration. The questions or statements to promote awareness are:

"You know me, who am I? Tell me about myself."

"Have we seen each other before? If so, where?"

"Now that you see me and hear me, am I what you expected? Are you surprised?"

To promote acceptance:

"When you were putting me together, I became aware of some important thoughts you were having. Remind me what those thoughts were."

"I like my colors. Why did you choose these particular colors?"

"I like my shape. Tell me about that."

To promote integration:

"What can I do for you?"

"What can you do for me?"

"How can we find each other when we need to?"

The video art therapy program can be carried out individually or in groups. We have tried the program with several individual clients and eight groups, with generally positive results. Hinz and Ragsdell (1990) used the program with a group of bulimic women, and experienced a high drop-out rate from the group. As with any innovative program, many more studies need to be carried out to ascertain how best to implement it and with which populations.

As a general rule, photographic and video images are confrontational. For that reason, the media must be used carefully and with respect for the impact that seeing one's own image can have. People suffering from psychoses are particularly vulnerable to such confrontation, and therefore are not good candidates for the programs we have presented in this book. However, Hartwich and his colleagues (e.g., Hartwich, 1986, 1987, 1989, 1990) have pioneered the use of video with schizophrenic patients and have met with some success. Their basic approach is to videotape the patient, and then to videotape the patient watching himself. The second videotape is then used as a focal point for a discussion between the patient and the therapist. Hartwich recommends keeping the self-viewing segments to only 15–30 seconds, in order to avoid overwhelming the viewer. Strictly speaking, such an approach is not an art therapy one, but does include the use of visual images.

Bowen (1990) has used photography in a Project Arts program in a day treatment center in Maricopa County, Arizona. The clients in the Center are mental health patients, some with severe mental health problems. In the Project Arts program, Bowen has clients take and print their own pictures. He believes that the photography classes help the clients make decisions, solve problems, and become more reality-oriented.

We have not discussed family photo art therapy in any detail. Corbit has used the Visual Transitions Group method (see Chapter Eleven) with the family as the group. The family constructs a poster using photographs of themselves depicting the dysfunctional family relationships. They then construct a second poster showing their photographs in some kind of ideal family structure. Both posters are constructed by the family members working together, resulting in considerable discussion and revelation of family dynamics.

Another family photo art therapy possibility is to have the family members choose one of Satir's communication stances (Blaming, Super Reasonable, Pleasing, Irrelevant, and Congruent) and to pose for a photograph in that stance. The photograph can then be used in much the same way as the other projects depicted in this book. The family members could develop a poster of the entire family, using the photographs, as in the chapter on group cohesion (see Chapter 12). We have not used this technique with families, but Cox (1991) has suggested it and tried it with student therapists posing as family members.

Denver photographer and therapist Katy Tartakoff (1991) is using photojournal workbooks to help children cope with life-threatening illnesses and trauma. She has designed two journals, *My Stupid Illness* and *My Life Journal.* Polaroid photographs of and by the children document their struggles with the medical treatment, the process of dying, and their hopes of recovery. In the workbook are creative activities that address self-concept, friends and family members, the emotions of happiness, sadness, fear, anger, and pride, and their understanding of the disease and the medical procedures. The journal assignments enable the children to express the truth through the media of photography, writing, drawing, and collage making. Cancer patients, AIDS patients, and burn victims have participated in her programs. Tartikoff has established a nonprofit organization to further the programs. She can be contacted at *The Children's Legacy Foundation,* P.O. Box 300305, Denver, Colorado 80203.

One more person we should mention is Judy Weiser. Weiser has established the PhotoTherapy Centre in Vancouver where she trains therapists in the use of photographs, and where she has a therapy practice. She has developed numerous techniques and has recently described them in a book (in press). One particularly interesting use of photographs is similar to the use of Rorschach Inkblots, or Thematic Apperception Test plates. Weiser has a collection of photographs on the walls of her office, and she has clients react to them, picking out the one that is the most emotionally arousing, or the one most interesting to the client. She then has the client respond to a series of questions about the photograph, thus projecting his own personality concerns into the situation.

In conclusion, there are interesting and innovative therapy methods using instant photographs and art as media, and we expect many more methods to be invented in the next few years.

Chapter 15

SUMMARY AND CONCLUSIONS

W e have become convinced over the years that the combination of instant photographs and other art media is a powerful therapeutic alliance. In this book we have attempted to give detailed examples of how the media can be combined in therapeutic ways, and we have tried to make theoretical sense of the therapy from the perspective of C. G. Jung's analytic theory. We hope the reader has come away from this book with several new therapy methods and some rationale as to why the methods can be helpful with clients.

Jung's assertions that we must become more knowledgeable about ourselves, including especially our unconscious dynamics, in order for individuation and transcendence to proceed, figure prominently in our work. In the first section of the book, *Self-Understanding*, we emphasized the importance of understanding ourselves, both our conscious deliberate motives and traits, and our unconscious personalities. We detailed methods for understanding oneself in relationship to nature, to other people, and to oneself.

In the United States, something like 75 percent of the people live on 3 percent of the land. In other words, we mostly live in cities. As urban city dwellers we have lost many of our connections to nature, without losing our basic yearning for the natural world. In Chapter 1 we made an argument for re-establishing these connections, using the photography and art media.

Without doubt we are social creatures. Our U.S. urban areas average 2,000 people per square mile. With such crowding, it is imperative that we get along with each other. Central to an ability to live peacefully with other people is our ability to understand ourselves. An understanding of ourselves has to include our basic orientations toward other people. Jung's theoretical concepts of extraversion/introversion and the anima/ animus are relevant, as are Adler's concepts of social interest and striving for superiority. Chapter Two was devoted to the use of photo art therapy in the understanding of one's relationships to other people.

Understanding oneself in relationship to oneself entails understanding the persona, that mask we present to the world. In order for us to really be comfortable with ourselves, we need to discard the persona and to be willing to risk showing our true selves to other people. Chapter Three was concerned with the persona and a technique we called the Self-Portrait Box, which investigated the persona we show and the private personality we hide.

Self-understanding also means becoming more acquainted and comfortable with the shadow side of the personality, that part of the personality that is dimly perceived by most people, if at all. The overriding consideration is that, if we are not acquainted with ourselves, then we are doomed to be driven by unconscious shadowy forces that may not be in our overall best interests. The more we know about ourselves, the more freedom we have from the tyranny of the shadow. Chapter 4 contained a rationale and methods for confronting and understanding the shadow.

Self-understanding also entails delving into Jung's concept of the archetypes, those underlying collective predispositions that he posed as the foundation of behavior. Collective archetypes are most noticeable in the cultural collections of art work, fairy tales, and folk tales. Much of our work with archetypes includes the use of fairy tales, combined with instant photographs and other art materials. Putting oneself into a fairy tale illustration, using an instant photograph, allows one to experience visually becoming an archetypal part of the story. Chapter 5 was a discussion of photo art therapy and the archetypes.

No book purporting to address analytic theory would be adequate without a discussion of dreams. In Chapter 6 we not only discussed dreams, but we gave specific instructions on carrying dreams on through Jung's method of active imagination, to attempt a resolution of the unconscious dynamics that make up the dream. The active imagination method, coupled with photo art therapy, can be very useful for people to better understand their dreams and to transcend them.

In Section Two of the book, we wrote four chapters detailing specific methods and theoretical rationale for dealing with psychopathological symptoms. We addressed fears, conflicts, depression, and the healing of the effects of child abuse.

Chapter 7, dealing with fears, was specifically targeted at work with children, although many of the methods could be used with adults. We also included photo art therapy combined with the sandplay method.

Intrapsychic conflicts lend themselves to resolution with photo art therapy. By posing for a photograph representing both sides of a conflict, a client can literally see the conflict and can work on a resolution using the art work as a referent. Chapter 8 was a discussion of this method of resolution.

In Chapter 9, we attempted a melding of Jung's analytic theory with Beck's cognitive theory of depression and its treatment. Specifically, we made the argument that cognition is not all verbal, it is also visual, and the visual components can be combined with the verbal in creative and therapeutic ways.

In Chapter 10, we report a case study of a woman who used the photo art therapy techniques to heal the wounded child within. Through several of the methods we detailed in previous chapters, the client was able to gain new perspectives on her abuse and graciously and courageously shared her art work and comments about it.

Section Three, *Group Therapy*, contained three chapters on group work. Chapter 10 was a description of a multimodal art therapy group method the authors have developed and named *Visual Transitions.* The method includes photography, video, movement, art, meditation, and discussion. Chapters 11 and 12 addressed the well-known problems of developing group cohesion and dealing with a stuck group. Photo art therapy methods were proposed for both problems.

In Chapter 14, we asked readers to be aware and concerned about confidentiality. The issue of confidentiality is of particular concern when therapists use photographs or video because people may recognize the faces of the clients. In Chapter 14 we included a list of art materials for photo art therapy and we also discussed briefly several other photo or video art therapy methods that we know about and that we find especially appealing but that do not fit neatly into any other chapter.

In conclusion, the photograph as an art therapy medium offers numerous advantages, especially when combined with other art media. The image is almost instant, and no artistic ability whatsoever is required. Polaroid cameras are easy to use, and the client can use photographs taken of her or by her in a multitude of creative ways, as we have discussed. We plan to continue to explore new ways of using the medium and feel sure that other people will as well. We expect to see new ideas that we have not yet imagined.

REFERENCES

Adler, G. (1948). *Studies in analytical psychology.* New York: W. W. Norton.

Afanasev, A. (1973). *Russian fairy tales.* New York: Pantheon Books.

Alger, I. and Hogan, P. (1967). The Use of Videotape Recordings in Conjoint Marital therapy. *American Journal of Psychiatry, 123,* 1425–1430.

American Art Therapy Association Ethics Committee (1988). Ethical Standards for Art Therapists. *American Art Therapy Association Newsletter,* Vol. XX, No. 4, 15–16.

American Psychiatric Association (1987). *Diagnostic and Statistical Manual of Mental Disorders — Third Edition — Revised.*

American Psychological Association Ethics Committee (1990). Ethical Principles of Psychologists (Amended June 2, 1989). *American Psychologist,* Vol. 45, No. 3, 390–395.

Beck, A. T. (1967). *Depression: Causes and treatment.* Philadelphia: University of Pennsylvania Press.

Beck, A. T. (1976). *Cognitive therapy and emotional disorders.* New York: International Universities Press.

Beck, A. T., Rush, A. J., Shaw, B. F., and Emery, G. (1979). *Cognitive theory of depression.* New York: Guilford Press.

Berger, M. M. (Ed.) (1978). *Videotape techniques in psychiatric training and treatment, Rev. Ed.,* New York: Brunner/Mazel.

Bowen, R. (1990). Personal Communication.

Bradway, K. (1982) Gender Identity and Gender Roles: Their Place in Analytic Practice. In M. Stein (Ed.) *Jungian analysis.* LaSalle, IL: Open Court.

Breuer, J. and Freud, S. (1895). *Studien uber hysterie* (Leipzig and Vienna. Translated as *Studies in Hysteria.* New York, 1936 and 1947.

Briggs, K. C. and Myers, I. B. (1977) *Myers-Briggs Type Indicator.* Palo Alto, CA: Consulting Psychologists Press.

Buchalter-Katz, S. (1989). "Barrier" drawings for depressed patients. In H. Wadeson, J. Durkin and D. Perach (Eds.) *Advances in art therapy.* New York: John Wiley.

Cohen, F. and Phelps, R. (1985). Incest Markers in Children's Artwork. *The Arts in Psychotherapy,* Vol. 12, pp. 265–283.

Corbit, I. (1985). *Veterans's nightmares: Trauma, treatment, truce.* Unpublished Doctoral dissertation. Ann Arbor, MI: University Microfilms, Inc.

Cornelison, F. and Arsenian, J. (1960). A Study of the Responses of Psychotic Patients to Photographic Self-image Experience. *Psychiatric Quarterly, 34,* 1–8.

Cox, K. (1991). Personal Communication.

Dollard, J. and Miller, N. E. (1950). *Personality and psychotherapy: An analysis in terms of learning, thinking, and culture.* New York: McGraw-Hill.

Edinger, E. (1972). *Ego and archetypes.* New York: G. P. Putnam's Sons for the C. G. Jung Foundation for Analytical Psychology.

Erickson, M. (1980). *The collected papers of Milton H. Erickson on hypnosis.* E. L. Rossi (Ed.). New York: Irvington.

Fisher, S. and Greenberg, R. (Eds.) (1978). *The scientific evaluation of Freud's theories and therapy.* New York: Basic Books.

Fleshman, B. and Fryrear, J. L. (1981). *The Arts in Therapy.* Chicago: Nelson-Hall.

Frey-Rohn, L. (1967). *Evil.* Evanston, IL: Northwestern University Press.

Fry, R. T. (1974). *Teaching active imagination meditation.* Unpublished doctoral dissertation. Laurence University California, Goleta, California.

Fryrear, J. L. and Fleshman, B. (1981). *Videotherapy in mental health.* Springfield, IL.: Charles C Thomas.

Fryrear, J. L. and Corbit, I. E. (1989). Visual Transitions: Metaphor for Change. In H. Wadeson, J. Durkin, and D. Perach (Eds.) *Advances in art therapy.* New York: John Wiley.

Fryrear, J. L. and Krauss, D. A. (1983). Phototherapy Introduction and Overview. In D. A. Krauss and J. L. Fryrear (Eds.). *Phototherapy in mental health.* Springfield, IL: Charles C Thomas.

Fryrear, J. L. and Price, K. (1991). "An art therapy transition program for children in protective care." Paper presented at "Current issues in mental health" conference, University of Houston-Clear Lake, Houston, Tx.

Fryrear, J. L. and Stephens, B. (1988). Group Psychotherapy using Masks and Video to Facilitate Intrapersonal Communication. *The Arts in Psychotherapy.* Vol. 15, 227–234.

Fryrear, J. L. and Stephens, B. (1990). Response to Hinz and Ragsdell. *The Arts in Psychotherapy.* Vol. 17, No. 3, 263–264.

Gad, I. "Beauty and the Beast" and "The wonderful sheep:" The Couple in Fairy Tales: When Father's Daughter meets Mother's Son. In M. Stein and L. Corbett (Eds), *Psyche's stories: Modern Jungian interpretations of fairy tales.* Wilmette, IL: Chiron Publications.

Greene, T. A. (1982). Group Therapy and Analysis. In M. Stein (Ed.), *Jungian analysis.* La Salle, IL: Open Court.

Hall, J. (1977). *Clinical uses of dreams: Jungian interpretations and enactments.* New York: Grune and Stratton.

Hall, J. (1982). Dream Interpretation in analysis. In M. Stein (Ed.), *Jungian analysis.* La Salle, IL: Open Court.

Hall, J. (1983). *Jungian dream interpretation.* Toronto: Inner City Books.

Hall, J. (1986). *The Jungian experience: Analysis and individuation.* Toronto: Inner City Books.

Hall, J. (1990). Presentation at International C. G. Jung Conference, Houston, Texas.

Hall, J. (1991). *Patterns of dreaming: Jungian techniques in theory and practice.* Boston and London: Shambhala.

Hartwich, P. (1986). Audiovisuelle Verfahren. In Chr. Muller, (Ed.), *Lexikon der perchiatrie*. Berlin, Heidelberg, New York: Springer.

Hartwich, P. (1987). Schizophrenien: Kognitive Gesichtspunkte. In K. P. Kisker, (Ed.), *Psychiatrie der Gegenwart*. Berlin, Heidelberg, New York: Springer.

Hartwich, P. (1989) "Audiovisual self-viewing experience in the therapy of schizophrenics." VIII World Congress of Psychiatry. Athens.

Hartwich, P. (1990). "Psychiatry in the treatment of schizophrenia with drawings and video-mirroring." International C. G. Jung Conference, Houston, Texas.

Heilveil, I. (1983). *Video in mental health practice: An activities handbook*. New York: Springer.

Hillman, J. (1975). *Re-visioning psychology*. New York: Harper and Row.

Hillman, J. (1983). *Healing fiction*. Barrytown, NY: Station Hill.

Hinz, L. D. and Ragsdell, V. (1990). Brief Report: Using Masks and Video in Group Psychotherapy with Bulimics. *The Arts in Psychotherapy*. Vol. 17, No. 3, 259–262.

Houston, J. (1982). *The possible human*. Los Angeles: J.P. Tarcher, Inc.

Jacobs, S. (1991). Personal Communication.

Johnston, J. (1978). Elements of Senoi Dreaming Applied in a Western Culture. *Sundance Community Dream Journal*, 2:1, pp. 50–61.

Jung, C. G. (1964). *Man and his symbols*. London: Aldus Books.

Jung, C. G. (1953). *Two essays on analytical psychology*. Collected Works, Vol. 7. Bollingen Series XX. Pantheon Books. Princeton University Press.

Jung, C. G. (1960). *The structure and dynamics of the psyche*. Collected Works, Vol. 8. Bollingen Series XX. Pantheon Books. Princeton University Press.

Jung, C. G. (1959). *The archetypes and the collective unconscious*. Collected Works, Vol. 9, Part 1. Bollingen Series XX. Pantheon Books. Princeton University Press.

Jung, C. G. (1964). *Civilization in transition*. Collected Works, Vol. 10. Bollingen Series XX. Pantheon Books. Princeton University Press.

Jung, C. G. (1963). *Mysterium coniunctionis*. Collected Works, Vol. 14. Bollingen Series XX. Pantheon Books. Princeton University Press.

Jung, C. G. (1966). *The spirit in man, art and literature*. Collected Works, Vol. 15. Bollingen Series XX. Pantheon Books. Princeton University Press.

Jung, C. G. (1954, 1966). *The practice of psychotherapy, 2nd. Edition*. Collected Works, Vol. 16. Bollingen Series XX. Pantheon Books. Princeton University Press.

Jung, C. G. (1955). *The symbolic life*. Collected Works, Vol. 18. Bollingen Series XX. Pantheon Books. Princeton University Press.

Kalff, D. M. (1980). *Sandplay: A psychotherapeutic approach to the psyche*. Santa Monica, CA: Sigo Press.

Kaplan-Williams, S. (1985). *The Jungian-Senoi dreamwork manual*. Berkeley, CA: Journey Press.

Keeney, B. P. (1983). *Aesthetics of change*. New York: The Guilford Press.

Kelsey, M. (1978). *Dreams: A way to listen to God*. New York: Paulist Press.

Keyes, M. F. (1974). *The inward journey: Art as therapy for you*. Millbrae, CA: Celestial Arts.

Krauss, D. and Fryrear, J. L. (1983). *Phototherapy in mental health*. Springfield, IL: Charles C Thomas.

Lambert, M. (1988). Personal Communication.

McNiff, S. (1987). Pantheon of Creative Arts Therapies: An Integrative Image of the Profession. *Journal of Integrative and Eclectic Therapy.* 6(3), 259–281.

McNiff, S. (1990). Hillman's Aesthetic Psychology. *The Canadian Art Therapy Association Journal.* Vol. 5, 1.

Melnechuk, T. (1983). The Dream Machine. *Psychology Today.* November.

O'Connell, W. E. (1981). *Essential readings in natural high actualization.* Chicago: North American Graphics. 1982.

Powell, L. and Faherty, S. L. (1990). Treating Sexually Abused Latency Age Girls. *The Arts in Psychotherapy.* Vol. 17, No. 1, 35–48.

Roberts, J. and Pines, M. (1991). *The practice of group analysis.* New York: Tavistock/ Routledge.

Roberts, R. (1983). *Tales for Jung folk.* San Anselmo, CA: Vernal Equinox Press.

Rogers, C. (1951). *Client-centered therapy.* Boston: Houghton Mifflin.

Rosen, S. (1982). *My voice will go with you: The teaching tales of Milton Erickson.* New York: W. W. Norton.

Samuels, A., Shorter, B., and Plaut, F. (1986). *A critical dictionary of Jungian analysis.* New York: Routledge Kegan Paul.

Sanford, J. A. (1980) *The invisible partners: How the male and female in each of us affects our relationships.* New York: Paulist Press.

Schutz, W. C. (1958). *FIRO: A three-dimensional theory of interpersonal behavior.* New York: Holt, Rinehart.

Schutz, W. C. (1978). *FIRO awareness scales.* Palo Alto, CA: Consulting Psychologists Press.

Seemann, E., Stromback, D. and Jonsson, B. R., Eds. (1967). *European folk ballads.* Copenhagen: Rosenkilde and Bagger.

Sidun, N. and Rosenthal, R. (1987). Graphic Indicators of Sexual Abuse in Draw-A–Person Tests of Psychiatrically Hospitalized Adolescents. *The Arts in Psychotherapy.* Vol. 14, pp. 25–33.

Singer, J. (1972). *Boundaries of the soul.* Garden City, NY: Doubleday.

Singer, J. (1976). *Androgyny: Toward a new theory of sexuality.* Garden City, NY: Anchor Press/Doubleday.

Spring, D. (1985). Symbolic Language of Sexually Abused, Chemically Dependent Women. *American Journal of Art Therapy.* Vol. 24, pp. 13–21.

Sullivan, H. S. (1953). *The interpersonal theory of psychiatry.* New York: W. W. Norton.

Tartakoff, K. (1991). Personal communication.

von Franz, M.-L. (1974). *Shadow and evil in fairy tales.* Zurich: Spring.

Wadeson, H., Durkin, J. and Perach, D., Eds. (1989). *Advances in art therapy.* New York: John Wiley.

Watzlawick, P., Weakland, J., and Fisch, R. (1974). *Change: Principles of problem formation and problem resolution.* New York: W. W. Norton.

Weiser, J. (1986). Ethical Considerations in Phototherapy Training and Practice. *Phototherapy.* Vol V, No. 1, 12–17.

Weiser, J. (in press). *The secret lives of personal snapshots and family albums: A practical guide to phototherapy.* New York: Brunner/Mazel.

Wolf, R. (1976). The Polaroid Technique: Spontaneous Dialogues from the Unconscious. *The International Journal of Art Psychotherapy, 3:* 197.

Wolf, R. (1978) Creative Expressive Therapy: An Integrative Case Study. *The International Journal of Art Psychotherapy, 5,* 81.

Wolf, R. (1983) Instant Phototherapy with Children and Adolescents. In D. Krauss and J. L. Fryrear (Eds), *Phototherapy in mental health.* Springfield, IL: Charles C Thomas.

Wolpe, J. (1958). *Psychotherapy by reciprocal inhibition.* Stanford, CA: Stanford University Press.

Yalom, I. (1975). *The theory and practice of group psychotherapy.* New York: Basic Books.

NAME INDEX

193

SUBJECT INDEX

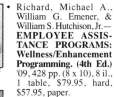
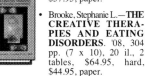